D0179289

RAISING A RESPONSIBLE CHILD

Revised & Updated

HOW TO PREPARE YOUR CHILD FOR TODAY'S COMPLEX WORLD

**Dr. Don Dinkmeyer
and Dr. Gary D. McKay**

A FIRESIDE BOOK

Published by Simon & Schuster

Fireside
Rockefeller Center
1230 Avenue of the Americas
New York, NY 10020

FIRESIDE and colophon are registered trademarks
of Simon & Schuster Inc.

Designed by Abby Kagan

Manufactured in the United States of America

1 3 5 7 9 10 8 6 4 2

Library of Congress Cataloging-in-Publication Data
Dinkmeyer, Don C.
Raising a responsible child: how to prepare your child for today's complex
world / Don Dinkmeyer and Gary D. McKay—Rev. and updated ed.
          p.   c.m.
           "A Fireside book."
    1. Child rearing.   2. Parenting.   I. McKay, Gary D.   II. Title.
           HQ769.D474   1996
           649'.1—dc20   96-20827
               ISBN 0-684-81516-8

To our wives, E. Jane and Joyce,
and our children and grandchildren

ACKNOWLEDGMENTS

WRITING A BOOK such as *Raising a Responsible Child* involves not only our own professional expertise and experience but also the influence and assistance of other people. With that in mind, we'd like to acknowledge the following persons with appreciation:

E. Jane Dinkmeyer, who not only shared in the parenting and grandparenting process but who contributed helpful editorial advice.

Don Dinkmeyer, Jr., Deborah Dinkmeyer, Jim Dinkmeyer, and Lyn Dinkmeyer, who contributed their practical parenting experience as well as support and encouragement to the grandchildren Luke, Joshua, Drew, Caitlin, and Stephanie.

Joyce L. McKay, Ph.D., who provided professional as well as personal assistance.

Robert Binz, Joyce's son and Gary's stepson, who exemplified a responsible child and is now a responsible adult.

Mary Bregman, Coral Springs, Florida, whose persistence, involvement, and support were invaluable, and who word-processed the manuscript through many drafts.

Rudolf Dreikurs, M.D., Bernard Shulman, M.D., Harold

Mosak, Ph.D., Oscar Christensen, D.Ed., Bill Hillman, Ph.D., and Kevin Leman, Ed.D., teachers, colleagues, and friends who influenced our work with parents, children, and families over the years.

Edward Abelson, Ph.D., Kevin Mathieu, M.Ed., and Barbara Mercaldo, M.Ed., who helped review and suggest ideas for parts of the book.

Finally, we'd like to acknowledge Betsy Radin, our editor, and the staff of Fireside for their assistance in this revision of *Raising a Responsible Child.*

Contents

>―·+‹›·―O―·‹›+·―<

INTRODUCTION: YOU DON'T NEED A LICENSE TO BE A PARENT . . . OR DO YOU?

D O YOU WANT to open a beauty shop? Get a license. Do you want to build houses? Get a license. Do you want to be a doctor, a lawyer? Get a license. Want to be a parent? Well, you guessed it. You don't need a license!

We want our hair to look right, we want our houses to stand up, and certainly we want good medical care, and if we need a lawyer, we want somebody with proven competence. If you want to be a parent, though, all you need is biology—right? True, but becoming an *effective* parent—now that's a different story.

It used to be that people didn't need training for parenting. We just did what came naturally, and things turned out okay— maybe. But not today, for sure. Sex, drugs, violence, and shifting family values are enough to make you think more than twice about having kids! But if you're reading this book, you probably already have them. So the question becomes: "Now that I've got 'em, what do I do with 'em?" Nobody ever prepared you to be a parent; they don't teach you in school. Oh, you may have taken a course in child development, but knowing how an average two-year-old behaves will not help you become an effective parent.

"Well, why not just do what my parents did? After all, I'm okay—or am I? And if I am, why did I buy this book? And why are there so many courses for parents offered in schools, churches, and mental health clinics these days? There must be something I need to learn."

Let us reassure you. Contrary to what you might think, there are very few "natural" parents in this world. Most parents face challenges from their kids that they don't know how to meet. Until recently, our society has not paid much attention to training parents. When we first wrote *Raising a Responsible Child*, in 1973, there were very few child-training books on the market. But check in any bookstore today and you'll find shelves and shelves.

So how come there are so many books, magazine articles, and TV talk shows and specials on parenting? If we just go back to the "good ole days," all our problems would be solved; we wouldn't need all this advice. The problem is, not everyone agrees on what were the good ole days. Some think it was the time of their parents; others, their grandparents, and so on. Ask a child of the 1960s who embraced the "love generation" and you'll get one answer. Ask a child of the 1960s who served in the Vietnam War and you'll get another. Ask women, ask minorities about the good ole days.

But there are some things on which most parents can agree: They would like their kids to grow up responsible, happy, caring human beings. They want them to be able to make a life for themselves and be responsible for their own support, not bounce back and forth to their parents' home like a rubber ball!

So how do we develop such qualities in our children? How do we raise responsible children? We can learn the following skills:

- Understanding their behavior and misbehavior. If we don't understand what motivates our children, we cannot be in a position to help them become responsible human beings. Attempting to do so would be like trying to fix a car without looking under the hood!

- Building their self-esteem through encouragement; helping them feel good about themselves and other people. Responsible people have high self-esteem and care about others. Encouragement applies to you, too. If you have low self-esteem, you will be in no position to help your kids.
- Giving them responsibility. To become mature adults, children must learn to assume age-appropriate responsibilities *as* they grow up. You can't expect a child to act responsibly at age eighteen if you haven't trained him from day one. But it's never too late. If you have a teenager who's not used to responsibility, you can still start to delegate tasks he's capable of handling—a little at a time. Sure, it would have been better if you had started earlier, but you didn't, and that's that—there's still time.
- Determining "problem ownership." Some problems you "own," and some your children "own." It's important to learn the difference. We can't help our kids become responsible if we assume ownership of the problems they can solve.
- Using natural and logical consequences, a disciplinary method that holds the child responsible for his or her behavior, not the parent.
- Listening to our children. We can learn a skill—reflective listening—that will help us really hear, and respect, kids' feelings and opinions.
- Sending "I-messages." We can learn how to communicate our feelings and opinions to our children and expect them to respect us.
- Exploring alternatives. We can help our children generate solutions to their challenges and thereby develop decision-making skills. Kids who learn to make good decisions become responsible. We can involve them in decisions that affect their lives. We can't, however, let them control the family, but we can permit them to share in those rules that affect it. We'll encourage you to hold regular family meetings to make plans and decisions as a family.

These are the skills you'll learn in this new edition of *Raising a Responsible Child*. If you've read the original version, you'll recognize some of the material; much of it has stood the test of time. But you'll also notice that we've updated the book to address some new challenges that we face today. More women work outside the home now than did in the 1970s, for instance. We have more single-parent families today. We have more stepfamilies. More drugs, more violence, and more problems with sex and young people exist today, and AIDS and teen pregnancy are enough to scare you to death!

You'll notice new topics, such as divorce, single parenting, and stepparenting. For example, we talk about the different family structures and how the ideas apply. If you're divorcing, how can you do what's best for the kids? If you're a single parent or live in a stepfamily, how can you meet the unique challenges of these situations?

Regardless of your family structure—original two parent, single parent, stepfamily parent—you may face challenges with your children in such areas as schoolwork, drugs, sex, and violence. Here are some of the topics we address in this new edition:

- Television and computer games: how to deal with sex and violence
- Schoolwork: how to encourage learning and deal with homework and teachers
- Peer relationships: how to choose friends and what to do about bad influences, peer pressure, dating
- Talking to your child or teen about sex: when to begin discussing sex, abstinence, AIDS and other STDs, and pregnancy
- Helping your child or teen stay off drugs: dealing with drug-use messages and teaching your child to say no to drugs
- Dealing with violence: gangs and peaceful ways to raise children

If you haven't read the original, this may be all new to you. Between this book and our parent-education program, STEP (Systematic Training for Effective Parenting), we've trained millions—yes, we said millions—of parents in these techniques. (For more on STEP, see Appendix C.)

Our work is rooted in democratic child-rearing practices. "What, you mean you advocate letting kids do everything they want?" No! That's permissiveness, not democracy. We live in a democratic society in which each citizen is expected to take responsibility for his or her own behavior. We aren't permitted to do everything we feel like doing. We have freedom, but it has limits, one of which is not interfering with other people's freedom.

The problem is, many parents try to raise children through autocratic methods. "Do what I say because I say so." Such an approach doesn't prepare children for responsible living in a democracy. (Truly responsible people have to know how to make their own decisions and accept the consequences.) Nor does the opposite approach: "Do whatever you want." Permissiveness raises spoiled brats who don't know how to cooperate. (They don't even consider the consequences of their decisions.) Autocratic parents raise some kids who can't make a decision without looking to an authority and others who rebel against any authority. Most parents are autocratic in some areas and permissive in others, and some are even democratic on occasion.

Democratic parents raise cooperative, responsible kids. How? By allowing them to make choices and holding them accountable for their decisions—which is what develops responsibility. Later in this book you'll learn about using natural and logical consequences for irresponsible behavior, a disciplinary system based on choices and accountability. Do we advocate that kids be given choices about everything? Of course not! The law says school-age children must attend school, for example. Kids don't have a choice about that. But when you're having trouble getting your child to prepare for school on time, there are opportunities to structure some choices and consequences to meet this challenge (more on this later in the book).

The information and skills you'll learn from this book are based primarily on the work of Alfred Adler and Rudolf Dreikurs. Both of us were students of Dreikurs, who was a student of Adler. We owe a great debt to our teachers. Our work is a tribute to them.

1

THEY DON'T COME WITH
A MANUAL: MAKING SENSE OUT
OF CHILDREN'S BEHAVIOR

Y OU'RE JUST GETTING involved in your favorite television show when your son, Sam, comes in with his report card. The grades are the lowest he's ever had. You are exasperated. You ask, "How did this happen? I thought you were studying each night."

> SAM: *Well, I sort of forgot, and besides, I don't understand the work.*
> DAD: *If I've told you once, I've told you again and again. Set aside time each night. Ask me if you need help. What's wrong with you? You know better than that.*

Parents are frequently puzzled by their child's behavior and seek practical ways to overcome the frustrations misbehavior presents. Although it is interesting and perhaps reassuring to know that Johnny is only "going through a stage," how can his parents survive their child's apathy or rebellion? An intellectual understanding of behavior is educational, but it does not help them deal with the behavior. Parents need a pragmatic method

that will improve their child's behavior and at the same time reduce their own stress.

Upon consulting with the family doctor, parents are often
told, "Don't worry; he'll grow out of it. Most children behave
like that at this age." Unfortunately, there is now much evidence
indicating that the child who is bad-tempered, nervous, or uncooperative does not necessarily "grow out of the stage." Instead, we are finding that behavior is patterned and predictable
and that the child truly is "parent of the adult."

Frequently the victims of confusing and inadequate information, parents have been told to be more patient by some and
tougher or more demanding by others. They are advised to be
more permissive or simply proficient at mirroring the child's
feelings. Most of these suggestions center around the child. But
in reality the whole parent as well as the whole child must be
considered. Transactions with the child necessarily involve the
parents' feelings, attitudes, and values. And as parents we cannot hope to influence our children unless we first change our
own coping methods and perceptions. This does not suggest a
total personality reorganization, but instead a development of
new procedures and approaches for parent-child relationships.
We strive not only to understand our children but to develop
better ways to communicate and relate in our effort to build future generations.

Our culture has moved from an autocratic tradition that im-
plied that the parents' word was incontestably correct and final,
through permissiveness that set few limits, and now to an attempt to raise children who have self-discipline and social concern. New democratic procedures, which require mutual
respect, frequently leave parents utterly confused. Their experiences as children in autocratic homes and schools have not
equipped them to function democratically. Parents are never
sure if they are too strict or too lenient, too demanding or too
inconsistent. They only know that what they are doing does not
produce more effective relationships.

Parents have practical questions. They want to know:

"Why is John so annoying? I never seem to be able to give him enough attention."

"Why does Beth always want to be the boss? She tries to control me and get her way. I feel as though I'm always the loser!"

"How can I cope with rebellion? What should I do when George is mean and vicious to me and to the rest of the family?"

"Can you help me with Susie? She doesn't participate in school or social life. No matter what I try, nothing works. I have just given up trying to get her involved."

Why is John so annoying?

Mrs. Peterson has four children: Sue, twelve; Ann, ten; Betty, eight; and John, five. She is particularly concerned about John. Unlike the girls, who are cooperative, amuse themselves, and are, as Mrs. Peterson says, "a joy to be with," John is very demanding of her attention and continually mischievous. It is little comfort to think that this is a stage that will pass, since she has had this problem with John for three years. Mrs. Peterson does not need generalities and reassurance; she needs specific help.

Possibly John's position in the family as the youngest and only boy explains his perception of himself as special. However, knowing this does not lead us to corrective action. We must examine some specific incidents that reveal the dynamics of Mrs. Peterson's and John's behavior.

> MRS. PETERSON: *I guess the most typical incident would be at suppertime. The girls all help set the table and prepare the food. This is when John chooses to tease them or interfere with their chores.*
> COUNSELOR: *What do you do when this happens?*
> MRS. PETERSON: *I've tried everything, but I'm usually so annoyed that I get after him and tell him what a bad boy he is. Sometimes I spank him.*

COUNSELOR: Does this help?

MRS. PETERSON: I guess not, because he's still misbehaving.

COUNSELOR: Do you give John any planned time when you play with him only or do something he likes?

MRS. PETERSON: No, not really. I guess I'm too tired and annoyed after having to fuss with him so much.

COUNSELOR: Does John have any jobs he does for the family?

MRS. PETERSON: No, he's really too young to do anything very well.

After further inquiry, the counselor is ready to make some suggestions:

COUNSELOR: It seems that John feels he is special and must be the center of attention. Perhaps he does this to keep you busy.

MRS. PETERSON: It certainly does keep me on the go.

COUNSELOR: Children become responsible by being given responsibility. Are there any chores you can have John do that he would enjoy?

MRS. PETERSON: I could have him set the table. He's often asked to.

COUNSELOR: That's a good idea. I'd also suggest that you and John pick a time that is strictly John's and do something both you and he will enjoy. If you do something only John enjoys, he will sense you're not interested. And you yourself will probably dread the activity.

MRS. PETERSON: We could play with one of his computer games after supper each night or before bedtime. Is that what you mean?

*COUNSELOR: Yes. Then he will know that he will
be spending time with you in the evening and
won't have to pester you for attention all day.*

In this brief vignette, we have explored the goal of John's behavior and described some concrete suggestions for improving the relationship between him and his mother. Too often, experts have complicated a problem by giving parents technical explanations, psychological jargon, and clarification of the causes of behavior instead of supplying corrective actions. Behavior is best understood when it is recognized that the child always makes decisions that serve his or her aims even though the child is often unaware of the purpose. As one becomes aware of the child's goal in each interaction, it is possible to understand, modify, and correct behavior patterns.

HOW EXPECTATIONS INFLUENCE BEHAVIOR

Behavior is always influenced to some extent by our expectations. What we anticipate has an influence on our behavior.

A major deterrent to more effective child training is our attitude toward annoying, uncooperative, and rebellious behavior. A social conversation among adults about their children reveals that parents routinely tolerate misbehavior as normal, with no expectation that anything can be done:

Joy Smith and Mary Patterson are discussing their children. Joy begins by indicating that Jack, age ten, is going through an awful stage: "He fights with his brothers constantly, his room is a mess, and his schoolwork is failing. He's just a typical boy."

Mary replies: "Oh, yes, I know just what you mean. Bill is about eight, but he's going through the same thing. All children have problems with their brothers and with school."

Let's look carefully at this dialogue. Joy describes behavior that is certainly distressing to her but explains it as a stage. (Follow-up interviews with a counselor usually reveal that Jack's "stage" has been going on for eight years!) In addition, Joy feels that misbehavior is to be expected from boys. Mary, typically, doesn't attempt to discuss it further. She, too, accepts lack of respect for order and uncooperativeness as par for the course. She is relieved to hear that her troubled relationship with her son is not unique and accepts his misbehavior as normal.

We have come to accept misbehavior as normal and despair of ever changing it. But the problem really lies in our faulty understanding of human behavior and our personal discouragement about ever functioning more effectively with our children. As long as parents are resigned to being victims, children will continue to be tyrants! Parents need to recognize that misbehavior is not merely a stage or phase. It may be common, but it is not to be expected or accepted.

Tyranny by children is evidence of an uncooperative, self-centered pattern of life. Like most behavior patterns, it can be modified and dealt with to the benefit of the child, parents, siblings, and the community. Children are not monsters by nature. But they do need understanding, guidance, and firm limits to learn to live with others successfully.

Parents who love their children will help them develop their "normal" capacities to be sensitive, caring, socially relating beings. They will also require them to participate in the give-and-take of social living. As a result of such guidance, these children will learn to be concerned not only with what they want to do with their lives but also with making sure that they contribute in some positive way to society.

HOW DID HE GET THAT WAY?
HEREDITY, ENVIRONMENT, AND THE SELF-CONCEPT

It is not uncommon for parents to attribute their child's misbehavior to a variety of unlikely sources. "Danny is temperamental, and we say he's just like Grandfather." "Becky is stubborn; she got that from her mother." It is recognized that children come into the world with varied and unique temperaments. Each child's style of reacting is a reflection of temperament. As we recognize and accept some aspects of our child's temperament, we become more effective in understanding and relating with our child.

Heredity establishes the developmental rate of the individual and determines basic assets and liabilities. Environmental factors significant in the child's growth include the family atmosphere, parent-child relationships, the family constellation and relationships between siblings, and the procedures of child training. Obviously, the factor over which parents can have most control is the method of child training. But it is also important to recognize the active role that children play in their own development. They decide how to use their potential and the environment and have the creative capacity to give personal meaning to events and to act according to their own perceptions.

The way in which children choose to function provides insight into their motives and purposes. The self-concept is the key to understanding uniqueness. Children are not robots that merely react to external stimuli; they make decisions. Parents learn that on one occasion being quiet and patient can be an effective strategy; at another time, it might only provoke resistance. Children have the creative capacity to assign their own meanings to their parents' behavior. If they feel they are being treated unfairly, they will act on the basis of their perceptions regardless of the objective facts.

Causes of behavior are of interest, but they do not determine practical corrective measures. If a child is the youngest, from a divorced home, or physically handicapped, we can certainly acknowledge these factors. But they aren't excuses to be used as an explanation! It is more important to note what the child has decided to do about such situations. All of us can recall knowing children who function well in such circumstances. Understanding the child's behavior requires recognition of hereditary and environmental factors, but correcting that behavior involves working with his perceptions, attitudes, and values.

UNDERSTANDING BEHAVIOR: BASIC ASSUMPTIONS

Some of the material provided for parents on child training has been based on the presentation of general principles. The parent knows something about the average four-year-old but has not been given enough information to enable him to apply it to his own four-year-old, who may be four physically, six mentally, and three emotionally. While it may be of intellectual interest to understand the average child, it is of greater practical value to comprehend individuality and to become competent at working more effectively with your child.

We believe that each parent will benefit from understanding certain basic tenets related to human behavior. These propositions will enable him to understand behavior and act more effectively in a variety of situations. Parents must learn how to expand their response repertoire with children as well as how to select responses that are effective.

The child is a social, decision-making being whose psychological pattern and style of life have a purpose. The following premises provide general guidelines for specific actions:

1.   Behavior is best understood in terms of its unity or pattern.

The child always responds as a total being with thoughts, feelings, and actions. Often we deal with the child's actions as if they were isolated, whereas they are actually part of a pattern. The parent must become familiar with the child's beliefs and assumptions about life. These provide the basis for the child's patterns of behavior, influencing the nature of the relationships the child forms and his willingness to accept responsibility. The child's behavior reveals his movement toward or away from the parent's expectations. The direction of movement influences the transactions between parent and child. This movement is described in the following example, which clearly reveals goals, purpose, and the meaning of behavior.

> Bill's failure to make his bed or clear the table may be related to his unwillingness to keep his desk at school clean or complete his assignments. His habitual failure to respond to order is part of his basic approach to life. He believes it is not necessary for him to cooperate and has learned that he eventually wears people down.

As his mother says, "It is easier to do it myself than to make Bill do it." True, it is easier if she is not concerned about helping the child mature. Parents who perform functions that the child can manage by himself are helping establish a basic pattern of dependency for life. Bill has learned that the consequences of his failure to respond to order may be a lecture or scolding, but in the end he gets his way.

The child not only reacts but interprets situations and decides. Experiences in the family atmosphere, particularly competition with siblings, are crucial in forming the child's perception of his experiences. The child's convictions, attitudes, and values are reflected through his lifestyle, which is a characteristic pattern of response to life situations.

2. Behavior is goal directed and purposive.

Often parents say, "Johnny's behavior just doesn't make sense. I've done nothing to cause that reaction." Johnny's parents will be able to understand their son's behavior if they approach it in terms of its results. Every psychological action has a goal, and this goal becomes the final cause of, or explanation for, the behavior. The individual's decision, displayed in his transactions with others, reveals his purpose; thus, the consequences reveal the purpose of the behavior.

> Betty, age five, appears to be bright, but she still needs much help in dressing herself. She is also afraid of the dark, and her mother must stay in her room each night

until she falls asleep. Let's look at the consequences, and hence the purpose and explanation, of her behavior. By being inadequate, Betty receives special service in dressing and at bedtime. She becomes a princess with a private servant. If her mother does not cooperate, Betty uses emotions—for example, crying—to restore her control of the situation.

Rudolf Dreikurs,[1] an eminent psychiatrist and a leading authority on democratic approaches, has classified the goals of misbehavior as attention getting, the struggle for power, the desire for revenge, and the display of inadequacy or assumed disability in order to escape expectations. Betty's demands on her mother manage to gain attention and power while she maintains a semblance of weakness.

The child who is overly concerned with attention getting usually prefers to receive it positively, but she will accept negative attention rather than be ignored. Unlike the child who strives for attention by becoming accomplished and industrious, the negative attention getter is most successful when she is annoying. In both cases, the child's behavior requires others to notice and deal with her. The child is a specialist at keeping mother and teacher busy with her, whether by praise or reprimand. In order to modify such behavior, it is necessary to ignore negative attempts to involve others while at the same time finding ways to give the child positive attention and recognition.

The power-seeking individual is out to show that he can control. He refuses to cooperate and will only do exactly what he wants to do. The most common mistake in dealing with such behavior is to attempt to enforce one's will, which usually only throws coals on the fire and stimulates a greater need for power. Eventual defeat actually stimulates the child to find a more cunning way to control. Parents must learn to avoid this most common reaction, for it is the behavior the child is anticipating; hence, their response actually reinforces the misbehavior. Kevin Leman, a psychologist and author,[2] had some ideas that are helpful in identifying and becoming aware that you are in a power struggle. You might identify how important it is for you to win. Do you feel it is essential that you don't lose the contest? Do you feel that your prestige and authority are being challenged? Most important of all, Leman suggests that your tone of voice is a good measure of your attitude. If you sound insistent and demanding, you're probably in a power struggle.

If the child's goal is revenge, he will seek significance by being cruel and disliked. To be called the worst or most horrible is his sought-after trophy. He enjoys mutual antagonism and feels best when others are hurt by him. The parent must recognize that his desire to retaliate contributes to the child's negative self-concept. When you become aware of revengeful behavior in your children, it is important to note it carefully and to be thoughtful about your actions. When a child has reached a revenge level that you experience as powerful, he is often on the road to becoming violent. Revenge is an advanced step in the child's level of discouragement. The revengeful child often believes: "I've been hurt or treated unfairly, and I have the right to get even and hurt them back." Avoid feeling hurt or seeking revenge. Instead, work to build a relationship of trust and acceptance.

The child whose goal is to display disability has developed an approach to life that prevents others from expecting anything of him. He is deeply discouraged, lacks faith in his capacities, and seeks to avoid any anticipation on the part of others that he will be productive and cooperative. The parent avoids all criticism and encourages and reinforces any effort by the child to change, no matter how slight. Focusing on strengths and assets is especially important to the child.

While these goals may seem complex, it is encouraging to know that any parent can learn how to identify the purpose of misbehavior by closely observing the psychological transactions and their consequences. Check your own spontaneous reaction to the child at the time of misbehavior. Your reaction will usually point to the child's intentions. When the parent is merely annoyed, the child seeks attention. When the parent feels challenged and wants to control, the child desires power. When the parent is hurt, the child's purpose is revenge. Finally, when the parent despairs and does not know how to get the child to function, it is the child's intention to display inadequacy in order to escape the parent's expectations.

GOAL	PARENT'S FEELING AND ACTION	CHILD'S REACTION TO PARENT'S ATTEMPTS TO CORRECT HIM
1. Attention	Parent is annoyed; wants to remind and coax.	Stops misbehavior; may repeat it later or do something else to seek attention.
2. Power	Parent is angry, feels defeated, threatened; tries to show child he can't get away with this.	Continues the misbehavior; stops momentarily and then repeats it; or does what he is told, but not to the parent's standards.
3. Revenge	Parent is hurt; wants to retaliate.	Retaliates either by intensifying the misbehavior or choosing another weapon.
4. Display of inadequacy	Parent feels like giving up, throwing up hands: "What can I do?"	Passively accepts whatever is done but does not improve.

After you have identified the child's goal by asking, "How did I feel?" and "What was my child's response to my attempts to correct him?" plan a course of action.

3.   The way in which the child seeks to be known reveals his self-image.

Each child, in a unique way, seeks a place in the family, among his siblings, and in the community. The reputation he tries to establish is derived from his personal perception of success, his self-ideal. We see this in the little boy who, in play, pretends he is a famous athlete. This can also be observed in the child who takes on the role of the cutest, the most helpful, or the most verbal. In some instances, the child may develop his reputation via negative traits, such as shyness, stubbornness, or cruelty. Whatever be chooses, he will want to be the best—the greatest athlete, the most helpful girl in the class, or the cruelest boy on the block. Because we live in a culture that emphasizes the value of being superior in contrast to being equal, the child develops a reputation that gives him status and then behaves in ways that establish and fortify this image.

The search for significance can motivate the scholar, the athlete, the singer, the ballet dancer, the bully, and the child who is valued because of his appearance or possessions. To understand and correct behavior patterns, it is vital to perceive the basic master motive or ideal that directs the child's lifestyle. Then the challenge in dealing with his misbehavior is to move it from passive and destructive modes to active and constructive patterns. This is accomplished by emphasizing the child's assets, building his self-esteem, and eventually redirecting his search for significance toward a more personally acceptable self-ideal.

4. All behavior has social meaning.

The child is a social being. His behavior is best understood when viewed in its social context. Always understand from the child's point of view how this behavior makes sense with a teacher, playmate, parent, or coach. When we empathize with the child and see his behavior in terms of his unique social environment, its meaning becomes clear. In most social transactions with peers or parents, the child is aware of the consequences and acts accordingly. As we have shown, it is not so bad to be scolded or criticized if you still get your way and get attention besides. All behavior is useful to the child. As you see how it makes sense, the purpose will be revealed.

In any given event, the child's psychological status and her perception of the meaning of behavior influence her actions. If she is the youngest and believes everyone is supposed to serve her, then she will behave with that expectation. If her experience indicates generally that people grant her special privileges, then these consequences will determine the course of her future interactions. She will only change as others fail to reinforce her faulty view of life and expect her to function more responsibly.

5. Each child has the creative capacity to make biased interpretations based on her perceptions.

It is basic to recognize that the child gives a subjective, personalized meaning to all transactions. She is regularly interpreting, evaluating, and making decisions about how to react in any given situation.

> Sally's mother calls her for dinner, and she does not come. She hears her mother but does not respond. Her mother calls a second time; Sally still does not answer. Finally, Mother screams and threatens, and this time Sally responds. Sally has learned that it is the third call that counts. When she hears the request, she determines, by the urgency and the tone of voice, whether it is a last call. From Sally's point of view, coming to dinner only makes sense when she perceives urgency and the possibility of unpleasant repercussions. Her mother's annoyance gives meaning to the event. Mother will learn that calling Sally once and letting her experience the logical consequences of failing to come (no dinner available) will be more effective than yelling.

6. The basic need is to actualize human potential.

Psychological equilibrium is a product of need satisfaction. Each child has the following psychological needs:

> to be loved and accepted;
> to be secure and relatively free of threat;
> to belong, to identify himself as part of a group;
> to be approved and recognized for the way in which he functions; and

to move toward independence, responsibility, and decision making.

As the child's needs are met, he attains an inner psychological stability. Failure to feel and perceive one's self as accepted, loved, secure, approved, and responsible are forces that stimulate misbehavior. The parent can always consider the need checklist when considering the reasons for, and the purposes of, misbehavior.

SOCIAL INTEREST

Child training, like any endeavor, requires certain long-range goals. In addition to a concern with developing his child's unique potential, interpersonal experience with the child makes the parent aware of the necessity for encouraging social interest or the child's capacity to give and take. The child with social interest is cooperative and respects the rights of others. He has a sense of his worth and a feeling of belonging. He is courageous in the pursuit of goals that reflect not only self-interest but social concern. Our goal as parents is to raise children who will be psychologically mature individuals, capable of adjustment, and, more important, able to contribute in a socially responsible manner. Learning to cooperate and work with people is essential in helping the child mature.

FAMILY INFLUENCES ON THE STYLE OF LIFE

Family Atmosphere

The child first learns to be human in the social unit of the family. The family provides the environment and the setting that expose the child to a set of assumptions about life. The commonly held traits, beliefs, and values arise from this atmosphere, as do the various means of relating to others. The child observes family relationships and exchanges and interprets them as the way to deal with other people. If his mother and father quarrel or if one of them uses temper or feelings to gain control, the child will observe closely and then adopt the procedures that appear to be effective.

Families that emphasize working together out of mutual interest will often stimulate the same behavior in their child. If the family as a whole values intellectual pursuits, music, or athletics, the children will often pursue those same interests.

The family pattern is not to be understood as a direct determinant of behavior. Obviously, the child is free to accept or reject the pattern. However, when siblings have similar character traits, it is frequently because they have internalized the family pattern. Differences in the personalities of siblings is a result of position and competition in the family constellation and of the individual's perceptions.

Family Constellation

Each child has a distinct position in the family. This position influences his perception of life. The ordinal position (actual numerical position as oldest, second, middle, youngest, or only child) frequently results in certain characteristic attitudes and traits.

The classic descriptions of ordinal positions usually suggest the following:

The oldest child is for some period an only child. Although eventually dethroned, she is concerned about continuing to be first. When she cannot be first, she may give up. If she cannot be the best in a useful way, she may decide to be the worst, which is another way of being first.

The second child may originally feel inferior to the older child. He will then compete and attempt to overtake a sibling. He will often appear to be working hard to catch up. If there is considerable competition between the two, the second child will usually become more of what the first is not, giving up in areas where he does not believe he can succeed. He may come to surpass the sibling in academics, athletics, or sociability, for example.

The middle child may feel deprived of the rights and privileges of the other children. She will either give up and feel that life is unfair, or she will succeed in overcoming both competitors.

The youngest child is the baby and can turn this position to his or her advantage. More often than not this child will establish a special place for him- or herself, frequently through characteristics that are passive and nonproductive. She or he may become the cutest, the most charming, or the most helpless. The youngest child can also become an active tyrant.

Because the only child spends his developmental years in the company of adults, he develops traits that win him the attention and assistance of adults. Thus, he may feel that he is equal in status to the adults and entitled to his own way.

Birth order is never considered to be a determinant. The child has the creative capacity to choose his role in the sibling order. His place in the family constellation provides clues, but we must always determine how the child has perceived and used his place.

Methods of Training

The child is significantly influenced by the methods of training employed by his parents. If the methods feature faulty approaches, such as spoiling, nagging, or excessive supervision, the child will not be allowed to experience consequences and will not learn from logical consequences. Protecting the child from the logical consequences of his decisions and actions by substituting nagging and punishment destroys the parent-child relationship and prevents the child from becoming independent and responsible.[3]

The following principles help the child become independent and responsible:

1. The parent understands the child and the purpose of his misbehavior.
2. The relationship between parent and child is one of mutual respect.
3. Parents are both firm and kind—the firmness indicating respect for themselves and the kindness showing respect for the child.
4. The child should be valued as he or she is. Assets and strengths are discovered, valued, and emphasized. Parents spend more time encouraging than correcting. One Positive Statement a Day is a good motto.
5. Parents learn to have the courage to live with their own inadequacies. They accept themselves as well as their child.
6. Parents learn to act more and talk less. Natural and logical consequences that teach a respect for order replace reward and punishment.
7. If a poor or ineffectual relationship exists, parents must have the patience and take the time to make corrective efforts. Developing human relationships that are mutually satisfying requires awareness but is worth the effort.

Parents play a major role in the formation of a child's lifestyle and personality. Their dialogue often directly affects the child's self-concept. Phrases that are negative and nagging, that point out faults, tend to promote feelings of inadequacy or resistance. Words that focus on assets, that are positive and encouraging, tend to build self-respect and self-esteem. The parents' real success and joy come from seeing the child emerge as an autonomous and independent individual who is at the same time secure enough to be responsibly interdependent with his parents and society. No job well done is ever easy. Being a parent must be "worked at"; satisfaction will follow. We believe parents need to focus on raising children who are responsible and cooperative, courageous, respectful and courteous, self-reliant, and able to see possibilities in problems.

2

BECOMING THE PARENT
YOU WANT TO BE

"Johnny, it's time to get up. You'll be late for school."
"Susan, here, let me help you get your blouse on."
"Marty, I've told you three times to come to dinner!"
"Brenda, don't forget your schoolbooks."
"Chuck, how many times do I have to tell you to take out the garbage? If you don't take that garbage out right now, no TV for a week!"

SOUND FAMILIAR? Nag, remind, serve, threaten—all the things well-intentioned parents do. Good intentions, faulty methods. We call such methods faulty because they take away the child's responsibility. Picture Johnny, Susan, Marty, Brenda, and Chuck as adults. Johnny learns that someone else is responsible for getting him up and off to school. Picture him and his wife several years from now—who gets him up and off to work? Susan may learn to button her blouse, but how many other dependent behaviors will she develop? Who nags Marty to get to places on time? Who becomes Brenda's memory? As for Chuck, will his boss remind and threaten him if he doesn't get his job done or just fire him?

The point is, simply, that responsibility begins when we allow children to be accountable for what they can handle. As you proceed through this book, you'll learn ways to help your child be responsible. For now, we want to discuss why parents take responsibility for their children. What do they believe about their role as parents?

THE CONTROLLING PARENT

The role of parent in our society is often misunderstood. A parent may believe that in order to be "good" she must dominate family affairs and be able to control the children. She may feel personally responsible for everything they do and act as if their misbehavior is a reflection on her parenting ability. This is not only discouraging to children; it's discouraging to the parent as well—society expects the impossible.

A controlling parent believes that everything he does is for the sake of his children. However, if his motives were truly altruistic, he'd be less concerned about his image as a parent and more devoted to promoting feelings of adequacy in his children. He'd try to stimulate a sense of cooperation and responsibility arising from within each child rather than applying external pressures that only prove his own self-worth. Children learn responsibility better by being given the chance to choose jobs that will contribute to the family than if they're assigned a task. Children's interest, the freedom of choosing, and their feeling of satisfaction with a job well done will help them attain the long-range goal of responsible adulthood and will make their parents' job of guiding them that much easier.

However, most parents feel insecure in their position. This is due to a society that is expert in discouraging its members. We're so mistake oriented that it's extremely difficult to learn from our mistakes in child training. The parent whose child isn't succeeding by the standards of the culture often considers this to be a reflection on her ability. Poor report cards, few friends, shyness, ineptness in athletics, aren't parental failures any more than success in these areas indicates accomplished parenting.

Many parents feel it's their job to protect their children. Of course, there are some situations in which a child is physically incapable of dealing with problems and needs protection. But areas of a child's life with which he can't cope are far fewer than most parents believe. A parent who overprotects views his child as incapable of dealing with life. His behavior reflects his own insecurity. He proves his worth by keeping the child dependent on him.

> *JAN: I can't tie this shoe.*
> *DAD: Come here, I'll do it for you.*
> *DICK: How do you cook the hot dogs, Mom?*
> *MOTHER: Never mind, the stove is dangerous. I'll do it.*

This type of protection keeps the child from growing up and maintains the illusion of the parent's great importance. The parent becomes the martyr, often complaining about how much she or he has to do: "See how I suffer." The real pity is that both parent and child lose in "smother love."

Controlling parents, then, may believe that they must control their children. They fail to see that attempts to do so often end in either rebellion or dependency. While parents are responsible for guiding children, doing so is different from controlling. Guiding parents focus on controlling the situation, not the child.[1] Controlling the situation means setting limits and allowing the child to choose within those limits. (See chapter 8 for more on limit setting.) The controlling parent attempts to force the child to comply with his or her demands. The guiding parent expects that the child will learn by experiencing the consequences of her behavior.

Controlling parents may believe that they're superior to children; they know what's best. This attitude puts children down by treating them as inferiors. True, you probably know more about life than your children, but acting as though you do doesn't improve your relationship. Guiding parents use their expertise to set up learning experiences for children.

> Jill, age sixteen, was on the school basketball team. The coach wanted the players to run three miles a day to improve their stamina and speed. Jill hated to run. Dad resisted the temptation to prod her. He figured that the coach had given her reasons why she needed to run.
> At practice before the next game, Jill had trouble keeping up with the other girls on the court. The coach removed her from the starting lineup.

Dad allowed Jill to learn from experience; if she wanted to play, she needed to follow the coach's instructions. He trusted her to learn for herself.

Some controlling parents want to please their children. They do it by providing special service. They may clean their children's rooms, provide a taxi service regardless of any inconvenience to them, pick up after them, and remind them of what they need to remember for themselves. Again, guiding parents structure opportunities for their children to learn responsibility.

The Effects of the Controlling Parent

The controlling parent affects each child in a unique way. In most families of more than one child at least one of the children stands out as more cooperative than the others. He's generally successful in approximating his parents' standards, and when he does step out of line, he is easily redirected. Most parents don't recognize the discouragement that prevails in this "good" child's life. He often feels he must be good in order to secure a place in the family. His efforts are directed toward impressing others and himself with his "goodness." He behaves cooperatively not solely to make life more pleasant but rather for the purpose of superiority: "Look how good I am."

But the "good" child does not necessarily surpass his siblings in all areas. For example, he may feel he can't shine academically and be the most congenial and cooperative at home; conversely, he may be an excellent student and completely irresponsible at home. In an effort to maintain his superiority, the "good" child avoids situations in which he feels he can't prove his "goodness."

The discouragement of the "good" child becomes quite evident when another child begins to improve in the areas in which the former maintains superiority. The "good" child often begins to slip; he may even become the "problem" child. This phenomenon of role reversal happens often, and it shocks and discourages parents. What they don't realize, however, is that the role reversal is actually a sign of progress, for now they have the opportunity to help the "good" child develop new relationships based on real cooperation and social interest rather than on superiority. By refusing to make comparisons and by encouraging any attempts to be mutually supportive, parents can now reduce the competition and strengthen the cooperative spirit between children.

A child who feels she can't secure a place through contributions and cooperation switches to the mischievous side of life to find herself a niche. The misbehaving child is very successful at gaining recognition from her parents. Although she'd probably prefer positive recognition, she chooses negative attention rather than be ignored: "If I can't gain my parents' approval, I can at least be important by making trouble."

Some children choose the role of the clown. The clown jokes continually and makes few contributions. He masks his feelings of inadequacy by making everything funny, keeping his parents upset and busy with him. At school the clown entertains his peers and at the same time annoys and frustrates his teacher by interfering with her attempts to teach. The reactions of his audience provide him with the recognition he desires.

Many children respond to their parents' behavior by choosing the role of the boss. The boss attempts to force others to give in to him. He strives to get his own way, often gets it, and only feels adequate when he's in control. He defeats his parent's efforts to get him to do anything he doesn't want to do. If she succeeds in forcing him, he does not perform to her satisfaction. He may try to retaliate for having to do what he doesn't want to do. In the classroom he defeats the teacher. He may refuse to study and learn, keep the classroom in turmoil, or bully his peers. His strivings for power are met with resistance, pressure, or compliance. And these reactions increase his desire for it.

Almost all children react to the controlling parent's standards and methods with some degree of discouragement. Since they can't live up to the parent's standards, they lose confidence in themselves and begin to feel inadequate. They become irresponsible, since the parent is busy being the responsible one. And they become defeated, since they find that they can do little that is good enough. Children may succumb to these feelings by resisting efforts to force their cooperation or by giving up, passively accepting whatever is done to them in the hope that they'll be excused.

Controlling parents are frequently victims of feelings of inadequacy, too, since they experience little success in influencing their children. They feel unappreciated, ineffective, and not respected. Both parents and children become expert at discouraging each other and accept their difficulties as inevitable.

If you want to become a guiding parent rather than a controlling one, you need to evaluate and reconsider your parenting style. Controlling parents are often autocratic, though some may be permissive. Few are democratic. In the introduction we briefly mentioned the idea of autocratic, permissive, and democratic parenting. We mentioned that most parents mix their styles, depending on the circumstances. For example, some parents will let their children do as they please as long as they don't interfere with the parents' rights or do something the parents consider wrong; then the boom is lowered. Let's examine parenting styles more closely.

WHAT'S YOUR STYLE?

This section was developed with the assistance of Ithaca, New York, psychologist Edward Abelson, Ph.D.
We've developed a chart to help you contrast the three styles. As you study the chart, you'll probably find that you employ a mix of styles—you're not alone!

Most parents, regardless of their style, want their children to behave responsibly and respectfully—and with consideration for others—and to follow a course that the parent thinks is in the child's best interest. The difference is in how a parent goes about influencing her child.

PARENTING STYLES[2]			
ISSUE	**AUTOCRATIC**	**PERMISSIVE**	**DEMOCRATIC**
Respect	Disrespects children, criticizes, blames	Disrespects self	Respects children and accepts them as they are; encourages mutual respect
Rights	Ignores children's rights	Ignores own rights	Respects all rights
Responsibility	Takes responsibility for all problems	Serves; takes on children's problems	Allows children to be responsible for their own problems
Methods to influence	Lectures, orders, threatens	Pleads	Gives choices within limits
Decisions	Makes all decisions; gives advice	Lets children do what they want	Involves children in decisions that affect them: explores alternative solutions
Response to misbehavior	Punishes: withdraws privileges, spanks	Reasons	Permits children to experience consequences of their decisions

The autocratic parent demands, the permissive parent begs, and the democratic parent sets up situations in which the child has a choice and an opportunity to experience the consequences of his or her decisions. In effect, the child discovers for himself what appropriate behavior is (dangerous situations excepted, of course). Here's an example of how the same challenge can be handled autocratically, permissively, or democratically.

Ten-year-old Charles and his pal Martin are running in the house.

AUTOCRATIC PARENT: Okay, boys, that's enough! How many times do I have to tell you that you're going to break something?
PERMISSIVE PARENT: Boys, please don't run in the house. You might break something or get hurt.
DEMOCRATIC PARENT: If you want to run, you'll need to go outside.

The autocratic parent gave an order and a lecture. The permissive parent pleaded and explained—something we're sure the boys already knew. The democratic parent assumed that the boys knew not to run in the house and simply gave them a choice. If the boys continued to run, the democratic parent would say, "I see you've decided to play outside. You can come back in when you're through running," and respectfully usher them out the door. The democratic parent used a logical consequence; in other words, he held them accountable for their decision. (You'll learn about logical consequences in chapter 8.)

Which approach do you think will be more effective if the boys decide to run in the house on another occasion?

As you can see, democratic parenting is *not* permissive. The parent sets the limits (sometimes with the help of the children, more on this later), but she permits the child to choose within those limits and to experience the consequences of his decision.

Both autocratic and democratic parents are leaders. The question is, what kind of methods do they use to lead? Autocrats boss; democrats guide. That's why we call them "guiding parents." It's your responsibility to set limits. In our experience democratic limit setting is more effective than autocratic bossing or permissive pleading with few or no limits.

Democratic parents have also been called authoritative. The authoritative parent uses his knowledge to structure opportunities for his children to learn cooperation. Tucson psychologist Bill Hillman calls democratic procedures "executive leadership." The executive leader structures, guides, and supports and expects accountability.

When things don't turn out the way the autocratic parent wants, she's often angry and engages in power contests with the child. She believes: He's to blame, and it's my job to straighten him out. To accomplish this, she escalates the conflict; she gives more orders, threatens, and punishes, which usually results in more intense rebellion from the child. The parent may eventually give up—temporarily—following the old adage He Who Runs Away Lives to Fight Another Day.

When things go wrong for the permissive parent, he tends to think, Poor child . . . it's my fault. He feels guilty and tries to make it up to the child. However, if the child goes too far, the permissive parent may feel hurt and angry and get even by reverting to autocratic methods. But he may feel guilty about that and return to being a doormat.

The democratic parent is likely to feel frustrated, wondering, What's wrong? I need to find another way to approach this problem. She doesn't believe in blame and fault, only in finding a solution based on mutual respect. However, the democratic parent isn't perfect. She can get angry and hurt, too, and she can feel guilty. When she does, she may revert to an autocratic method and may sometimes be permissive when she has no clue about what to do.

The difference is in the basic attitude of each parent. The autocratic parent believes he has to be in control. If he isn't, the children won't turn out "right." The permissive parent doesn't think she has any control—or should have. The democratic parent believes in controlling the situation, not the child. Each parent will work toward what she believes is the basis of her relationship with her children. When she slips, she'll work to get back to her style of relating.

WHAT KIND OF PARENT DO YOU WANT TO BE?

Now that you've had an opportunity to consider the three parenting styles and to see where you "fit," you have to decide what kind of a parent you want to be. Your choice is based on what you want for your children and how satisfied you are with your relationship with them. We're assuming that you're reading this book because you're not totally satisfied with your relationship with your children. A lot of people buy parenting books hoping that they'll learn some new tricks to make their children behave. If you haven't gotten the point yet, let us make it very clear: *The only person you can change is yourself.* The good news is that once you change your behavior, your children will most likely change theirs. Why? Because there'll no longer be a payoff for bad behavior. Remember the goals of misbehavior you studied in chapter 1? If you adopt a new way of responding to their misbehavior based on what *you* will do, not what *they* will do, they'll most likely adapt. We say "most likely" because there are no guarantees, since human beings are imperfect. But your chances of winning your children's cooperation are much greater if you concentrate on changing your own behavior than if you keep trying to alter theirs. But do realize one thing: *Your children's behavior may get worse before it gets better.* "Oh, no!" you say. Again, remember the goals of misbehavior? Your children are used to getting paid off for misbehavior. Once you decide to change, they'll attempt to pull you back into familiar territory. If you persist, however, they'll learn that the behavior will no longer pay off, and they'll most likely choose cooperation to gain your involvement.

The democratic approach holds the most promise for influencing your children for the following reasons:

- You involve them in decisions that affect them. Children are more likely to cooperate if they play a role in deciding.
- You permit them to choose within limits and to take responsibility for the consequences of their choices.
- You promote mutual respect. When parents show respect for children, and themselves, the children are more likely to respect them.

Essential in influencing anyone toward positive action is respect for the individual. Most of us lack respect for our children. We often talk *to* them rather than *with* them. Talking to someone implies that he's inferior; it automatically shows disrespect. The parent must try to talk with his child in the same manner as he would a good friend.

Also, many of our training procedures with children show disrespect. Parents punish, yell, remind, coax, and generally treat children as inferiors. Often, when parents do things for children that they can do for themselves, the implication is that they aren't capable persons. Parents often help children feel inadequate by criticizing their efforts just because the job isn't done as well as an adult could do it. Parents invade their children's privacy by prying into their thoughts and interfering in their affairs.

When dealing with his child, a parent can show him respect by taking his feelings and opinions into consideration before acting. When a child feels respected, he himself tends to be respectful and cooperative.

Okay, let's say that you've decided to become a democratic, guiding parent. Some other things you must do to develop that style follow:

PROVIDING A HEALTHY ATMOSPHERE

Too often the atmosphere of the home is charged with hostility between parents and children. Autocratic methods that fail stimulate frustration and defeat and promote ill feelings toward the child. The child resents the parent's efforts to control and deny the child her rights, and cooperation is misunderstood as giving into parental demands. If the parent trains the child to be highly competitive, then cooperation may even be considered a sign of weakness. Both parent and child feel trapped in their dilemma.

To provide a healthy atmosphere, which facilitates growth and cooperation, the parent must learn to accept and respect his child, to treat him as an equal person entitled to basic human rights. Being equal doesn't mean being the same. You're not the same as your children, spouse, friends, neighbors, but you're equal to them in terms of human worth and dignity. That's what we mean by equality, not sameness but of equal worth as humans.

The parent learns to listen to and encourage his child, to promote a sense of responsibility, and to set limits in a democratic fashion.

ACCEPTING CHILDREN AS THEY ARE

The first step in establishing a healthy atmosphere is to accept the child. This does not mean condoning all behavior. It's possible to disapprove of certain conduct without rejecting the child as a person. Tone of voice and manner must imply that the person is valued even though the present act isn't. It's essential to separate the deed from the doer. Consequences, for example, must be applied in the spirit of friendliness.

> Jack has put finger marks on the walls. Trisha, his mother, is bothered, but she wants to be respectful. "I see you had an accident; we'll need to take care of this. When will you clean the walls?"

The ability to accept the child is influenced by several variables. How you feel about yourself, and circumstances in your life at any given moment, will affect your acceptance of the child. Also, the specific situation in which a particular behavior occurs influences acceptance; that is, some behaviors that are tolerated when only the family is present may not be acceptable in the company of others.

In addition, some behaviors, and some children, are easier to accept than others. Parents who attempt to fool themselves with the notion that they feel, or even should feel, equally accepting of all their children often become anxious when they try to accomplish this extremely difficult, if not impossible, task. It's hard to feel loving toward someone who keeps "kicking you in the shins." Parents need to admit this to themselves and stop playing the "I should feel" game. Doing so keeps the parent in turmoil and hampers the establishment of a more satisfying relationship.

Once you recognize that acceptance varies, you'll be in a position to begin expanding the areas of it. This is accomplished through developing a more consistently positive approach toward the child. We're not suggesting that you become completely consistent; that would be impossible. We do suggest, however, that you become aware of the significance of consistency.

It's interesting to note that as you become more accepting of your children, they'll reciprocate. Children who previously "hit you when you were down" will become more considerate of your feelings and rights.

Accept the fact that the child is slow in reading or that it's hard for him to get acquainted with people—accept and value him. Don't nag; instead, encourage every small, positive step.

ENCOURAGING INDEPENDENCE

Permitting the child to make his own decisions is difficult for the parent who tends to be overprotective. When a controlling parent proves her worth through service to her child, she resists allowing him to become independent. The more self-sufficient he becomes, the less he will need her, and the less essential and worthwhile she'll feel.

Inhibiting the child's independence robs him of his security and self-confidence—two necessary and fundamental qualities for facing life—while encouraging the child to be independent helps give him the freedom to move in ways that permit cooperation and contribution. As an independent individual, he'll approach his social tasks with the attitude "What can I offer?" rather than "What will I get out of this?"

To foster independence, the parent permits the child to experiment and develop her capabilities. By trusting his child, he can communicate his faith in her ability to function. The parent who is interested in promoting this quality looks for every opportunity to encourage independence, refraining from making decisions that are in the realm of the child's abilities. If the child tries to evade independent decisions, the parent can respond with "It's your problem. I'm sure you can handle it."

As the child grows, there are many opportunities for independent functioning. An infant begins to become independent when the parent learns to allow the child to cry when there is no real need for her service. He soon discovers that his parent doesn't exist solely to cater to his every whim. As he becomes older, he must assume responsibility for his belongings and his room, and he must be allowed to dress and feed himself. When he enters school, he becomes responsible for getting up and off to school. Schoolwork also becomes his responsibility. In the child's relations with siblings, peers, and other adults, the parent follows a policy of noninterference. In this way, the child learns to give and take. The child is given an allowance and permitted to learn how to budget. He can choose his friends, clothing, and recreational activities. As a teenager he becomes responsible for discriminating use of the family car, dating, choosing courses of study, colleges, and professions.

Allowing the child to make his own decisions doesn't preclude the need for parental guidance. Through friendly discussion the parent can help the child explore alternatives. He'll learn to function adequately when he experiences the consequences of his decisions.

AVOIDING PITY

One of the most damaging of all human emotions is pity. Feeling sorry for the child, regardless of the circumstances, implies that he's weak and robs him of the courage needed to face life. The child who is pitied eventually learns to rely on self-pity as a way of avoiding difficult situations. He may even attempt to get others to feel sorry for him, hoping that they'll solve his problems for him.

There are many situations in which adults find it very difficult not to feel sorry for children. The parents of children with long-term illnesses or handicaps tend to want to make up for such difficulties by becoming oversolicitous. But the handicapped child is hindered much more by parents who pity her than by the physical or mental challenge. Such a child must learn to cope with life to the best of her abilities despite the challenges. She needs support and encouragement, not pity, to cope with life successfully.[3]

Poverty, divorce, or the death of a parent is often thought of by parents as a traumatic experience that causes other problems for the child. Although these happenings are certainly tragic, they don't necessarily have to be traumatic. The trauma is produced by the way the parents handle the event rather than by the event itself. If the child is pitied, then it's highly likely that he will suffer even into the future. On the other hand, if he's shown empathy, understanding, and support, he'll learn to overcome his misery and be able to handle subsequent misfortune.

It's important to distinguish between pity and empathy. Pity communicates "You poor helpless child"; empathy, however, communicates "I understand."

We help the child face disappointments by recognizing and communicating that he's disappointed but treat disappointments as a fact of life. When tragedies occur, help him plan ahead instead of dwelling on the tragedy. Get him involved; keep him busy. And parents must watch their own behavior, for children look to adults as models when tragedy strikes.

CHANGING YOUR ROLE

Parents can usually change their role in the interaction with the child without changing their basic personality. Most parents don't require therapy; they only need to learn more effective behaviors. Most of us have within ourselves the essential abilities necessary to change our roles.

When a parent decides to change his approach to his child, he usually goes in all directions at once and creates more problems than he solves. To avoid this trap, it is suggested that the parent work on one area at a time.

It's wise not to attempt to solve your most serious problem in the beginning, for often the area the parent finds the most difficult to change is closely related to his own uncertainty, values, and attitudes.[4] Instead, choose any area where success is likely. Recognize that when your child misbehaves, he expects you to nag, lecture, threaten—in other words, talk. Therefore, a good place to begin is to restrict meaningless discussion. Then, when improvement is satisfactory in this area, move on to another, and so on.

It's interesting to note that as you work through problems with the child, other areas of concern begin to correct themselves. As you improve your relationship with your children, they naturally develop the desire to cooperate.

The Desire to Change—Courage and Commitment

Changing behavior basically requires two qualities: courage and commitment. If you're courageous and really believe what you're reading is what is needed for yourself and your children, then your chances for success will be fairly good. If, however, you lack courage, are afraid to fail, or are not certain that this approach is for you, your chances will be quite slim. Commitment involves taking specific principles and executing them as consistently as possible.

Harry continually cried each time things didn't go his way. His mother usually tried to talk him out of crying with explanations and preaching. This approach usually intensified the crying to the point where Mother would become angry and send Harry to his room.

Mom decided to change her approach. She made a commitment to leave the room whenever Harry began to turn on the "water power." If Mom couldn't leave the scene, she busied herself with other thoughts or tasks. Before too long Harry stopped his crying jags because he discovered that his efforts failed to get his mother involved.

The qualities of courage and commitment lie within each of us, and they can be brought to the fore, but we must decide.

Refusing to Be Overconcerned About What Others Think

Perhaps one of the strongest stumbling blocks to change is over-concern about others. Parents often comment that they'd be unwilling to change a certain behavior because of what their neighbors, their child's teacher, or their own parents would think. It's important to recognize that those who look down on an individual are really expressing their own insecurity. If one felt secure, he'd have no need to criticize what others do as long as their behavior didn't infringe upon his own rights. When parents realize this, ignoring the opinions of others becomes less difficult. There comes a time for an essential decision: Which is more important to me, the opinions of others or my child's welfare?

THE EFFECTS OF YOUR NEW ROLE

When parents utilize positive democratic approaches, the results of their efforts are quite different from what is generally produced by authoritarian methods. A child who feels accepted, respected, appreciated, and useful develops feelings of adequacy that influence her attitude and behavior. She enjoys being responsible and becomes interested in cooperation as a means of gaining a sense of belonging. She's generally people oriented and interested in how she can contribute.

Cooperation and contribution stimulate positive feelings in an individual. It feels good to know one is able to help, and these feelings of usefulness in turn promote more cooperative behavior. A person who feels adequate has social interest and is more concerned with the welfare of the group than with personal gain. His motives are more altruistic than personal. He realizes that he's only one member of the group and that each person is equal. In the home he's concerned with his total family's happiness and well-being.

A child who is raised in a healthy atmosphere becomes self-sufficient and independent. He's prepared to meet life and its demands by "standing on his own two feet." He has the courage to try and isn't afraid of failure. When mistakes are made, he's not defeated; he's able to pick up and start again. Through his courage and self-confidence he increases his ability to handle difficulties and make responsible decisions. Above all, he's a happy person, enjoying life and all that it offers.

EXPLORING YOUR GOALS
FOR YOURSELF AS A PARENT

If you don't know your goals for yourself as a parent and what you want for your children, you're not in a position to influence. In other words, if you don't know where you're going, you'll never get there!

Most parents have some vague idea of what kind of a parent they want to be, though they probably don't think about it all that much—except when they make a mistake. Have you ever said, "Oh, no, I sound just like my mother [father]!"? Many adults want to be just the opposite of their parents and end up being just like them at times. But others want to be just like their parents; they think they raised them just fine. If the truth be told, most are some combination of their parents.

Take a few minutes to list your goals for yourself as a parent. Make the goals specific. For example, instead of "I want to be more democratic," list democratic behaviors, such as "I want to listen more," "I want to encourage," "I want to stop nagging, reminding, threatening, etc." After you've finished listing your goals, rate on a scale from 1 to 5, with 1 being the lowest score and 5 the highest, how well you're doing right now. Do this over the course of several weeks, rating your progress once a week.

3

ENCOURAGEMENT: THE BASIS FOR SELF-ESTEEM AND POSITIVE BEHAVIOR

ENCOURAGEMENT IS ONE of the most important parenting skills you can have. Developing it will help you become more effective in relating with your children. Misbehaving children are discouraged children; they do not have courage, self-confidence, or self-esteem.

Too often, parents harbor an idealized image of what their child should be and how he or she should perform. None of the standards, values, and goals we set for our child can be achieved until the child feels adequate and valued. Self-worth is basic to functioning as an effective human being. Parents are very concerned with identifying and focusing on the child's weaknesses and liabilities. Their intentions are good; it is only their methods that are inappropriate and ineffective. We need to recognize that we can't change a person's behavior unless we first change our expectations. There is considerable power in our interpersonal relations with children. Too often we use it inappropriately. We indicate to children both verbally and nonverbally: "I guess you won't make it; I suppose it's too hard for you. That's not the right way; I'll do it for you."

Fred, nine years old, has been assigned two jobs, making his bed and setting the table. He seldom cooperates, and his mother openly complains to his father, "Fred can't be counted on to do his jobs; I usually have to do them for him." The message Fred receives is "I'm not dependable," and the consequence is "If I don't function, Mother will do it for me."

Fred doesn't believe he can find his place in the family or feel adequate by behaving as his parents expect. His faulty assumptions and private logic tell him that if he misbehaves, at least he will be noticed and not ignored. His parents' goal, then, must be to build Fred's self-esteem, his courage to try, and his feelings of adequacy so that he will believe in himself and be willing to make an effort.

Encouragement involves almost unlimited acceptance of the child as a person. The encouraging person identifies assets and strengths and refuses to become overconcerned with liabilities. Encouraging parents appreciate a full and complete effort, but they are equally pleased to recognize any partial, positive effort on the part of the child. Encouragement is based on a belief in the innate capacity of people to overcome the challenges of life if they have the support that is so important to them.

The encouragement approach requires that parents be courageous. The purpose in pointing out mistakes is not to fault you as a parent but to help you understand mistakes and indicate ways in which you can change. Even if you change, you must realize that you will not be the "perfect parent." You need the courage to recognize that many times after a particularly difficult incident you will sit and reflect, That probably was the worst way to handle the situation. However, the way in which you deal with your mistakes has much to do with your effectiveness. In essence, you cannot encourage a child until you can accept yourself and begin to build your own self-respect and self-esteem as a parent. You will be most encouraging once you have developed your own courage, self-respect, confidence, and feeling of worth.

DISCOURAGEMENT

In order to properly understand the place of encouragement in child training, you must know the significance of discouragement. Discouragement is always based on your evaluation of yourself in a situation. A discouraged self-evaluation occurs when a person feels fearful, anxious, and inadequate. Those beliefs and attitudes result in limited courage and will influence future interaction with others.

The discouraged child believes there is little possibility of solving problems or even of moving toward a solution. The child lacks confidence and approaches each challenge with the anticipation of either a poor performance or failure. Recognize that the convictions underlying discouragement are based on over-concern with status and prestige. If the child is preoccupied with a need to be in a superior position, then obviously he or she will regularly be discouraged and dissatisfied. The antidote for discouragement begins with the courage to be imperfect, the acceptance of your limitations and failures. This means that the parent must help the child identify natural human imperfections and learn how to live with them.

It is the parent's duty to know the nature of the forces within the family atmosphere and the family constellation that stimulate discouragement. These forces include:

1. High standards. The setting of increasingly difficult standards makes success impossible and discourages the child; for example, the child who gets all C's on a report card is now expected to get all B's; the child who gets all B's is now expected to get all A's; the child who plays the piano reasonably well is now expected to become an artist.

2. Sibling competition. Parents, often unintentionally, pit the siblings against each other by comparing the excellent performance of one with the poor performance of another. Siblings have a significant impact on each other, and in our culture the social competition between them can result in severe discouragement.

3. Overambition. Overambition is a product of excessive standards. Overambition, the desire to be the best, appears to be positive until you recognize how many children give up rather than be ridiculed by peers for trying and failing. Other children may believe, If I can't be the best, I will give up and be the worst. If one carefully examines what appears to be a preference for certain activities, it becomes clear that this is more the result of discouragement in other areas than an actual free choice. In other words, a child may become extremely talented in music as a result of discouragement in competing in athletics or academics. This type of compensation has its advantages, of course, but the child ought to be able to accept, courageously, that one can enjoy a sport or music even if one is not outstanding.

Overambition can be observed in the child who refuses to join the game because he doesn't play ball well. If a child can't excel constructively, he may switch to excellence in rebelliousness or become "the biggest nuisance . . . the most passive student I've ever had" or "the shyest child in the family." These are the products of overambition and a competitive culture that values position and status more than persons.

METHODS OF ENCOURAGEMENT

The key to encouragement is in the child's understanding of what you are saying and your intentions. When you are encouraging, the child feels accepted and valued, has a sense of belonging, and is courageous and capable. If the child is not confident and courageous, you may have mouthed the words, but you have not communicated the feeling. When you encourage, you supply the methods for creating self-confidence and self-esteem. Courage enables the child to try again, to make the effort and persist.

Our typical methods of child training focus on overprotection, keeping the child dependent, setting unrealistic standards, and stimulating competition. These factors are almost guaranteed to produce a discouraged child. Instead, learn to talk less and to no longer make negative comments. Of course, there will be times you will be displeased with the child's actions. Make it clear to the child that while you don't approve of the action, you still value the child as a person. In effect, you communicate: I don't like what you are doing, but I do like you.

The basic methods of encouragement include the following:

1. Valuing and accepting the child as he or she is. We can build self-esteem only as we sincerely value the total person. This means accepting the child just as she is, with all her faults. Although you may believe you are valuing the child and may actually be communicating it to her, often your nonverbal cues, such as tone of voice, actions, expressions, or even a glance, are all signals to the child that she isn't living up to your expectations.

It is vital to separate the deed from the *doer*. When the child doesn't perform in the way you expected, help her understand that the failure was due to a lack of readiness or ability. In no way does this reduce her value as a person.

Billy has been playing Little League baseball. Father is very ambitious athletically and has spent a lot of time helping Billy learn to hit and field. He seems to do well when Father is practicing with him, but during games he becomes extremely nervous. After one game in which Father watched him strike out twice and make several fielding errors, Billy and his father were extremely discouraged.

> BILLY: *We really got bombed in that game, and I was the worst one.*
> FATHER: *You feel it was a very poor game.*
> BILLY: *Not only that—I was no good.*
> FATHER: *I guess it seems as if nothing went right, but remember, this is your first year.*
> BILLY: *I'll never be a star like Jack.*
> FATHER: *Maybe not, but you did field several balls well, and you hit a good solid drive to second base.*
> BILLY: *Will you still practice with me?*
> FATHER: *Certainly—it's fun for both of us.*

Father separated the deed from the doer. He took the time to point out the good aspects of Billy's play, the balls he did field, the valuable part he played in the general teamwork.

Sometimes when discussing a child's performance you can stress you are pleased with him as a person by stating something like the following: "You made some mistakes, son, but look at the way you . . ." This technique of turning the "but" around lets him know that it is okay for him to make mistakes and that his parent's real interest is in what he accomplished successfully. This, incidentally, will be quite different from the faint praise many receive before a "but" that introduces the complaint.

2. Using words that build the child's self-esteem and feeling of adequacy. Parents seldom recognize the significance of their verbal interactions. You have considerable capacity and countless opportunities to build the child's feelings of self-respect and adequacy by giving recognition and approval to any accomplishment or effort. When the child is facing a particularly difficult task, you can help by instilling the attitude "You can do it." Even if the results aren't successful, make sure the child is aware he or she is valued.

Often children will be in school recitals, contests, or athletic events attended by parents. At times when the child doesn't meet with success, the parent should relay some of the following attitudes to the child:

I was really pleased to be there and be your parent.

I am glad you played and participated.

While everything didn't come off as you hoped, I felt you made a good effort.

I can see you have made progress.

There are no failures, only outcomes.

Everybody makes mistakes. Mistakes help you learn.

MISTAKES

Science has enabled us to inoculate the child against a large variety of diseases. There is no such magic formula to protect against failure and unhappiness! Parents who apply the concepts in this book can build the child's self-esteem and self-confidence.

3.   Showing faith in the child so that belief in self develops. The child must feel she is an important member of the family and is worth more than any of the problems that are experienced. For example, in times of economic troubles, parents may complain about what it costs to feed, clothe, or educate a child. This may cause the child to wonder if she is really valued in light of all the complaining.

Parents often hold the child accountable for past failures and may feel prejudged. From the child's point of view, there is no way to change his or her reputation. Parents say, "I know that the last time you had a dog you didn't walk him, so I don't think we can get you one again," or, "When you tried dancing class, you lost interest, so I don't think I'm going to be able to support guitar lessons."

In many instances you need to forget past failures. Begin by helping the child believe in his or her abilities. Have the courage to permit the child to start with a clean slate. Remember the child's past successes, not mistakes. Remember, whenever you are trying to get the child involved and motivated, you are involved in attempting to change the child's anticipations and expectations. However, the child's anticipations will not change if you are already so discouraged that you believe the child will not make a full effort.

Sometimes parents are so cautious with things they own that they underrate the child's capacity to function. For example, the parent buys new china dishes instead of plastic ones. Now the parent is not willing to let Janet help her with the dishes. The parent explains that they should wait until Janet is a little older and less likely to break them. Janet's parents must consider whether it is more important to have broken dishes or damaged courage. Our observation indicates that broken dishes can be repaired and replaced much more easily than redeeming a child whose courage is broken.

4. Planning for experiences that are guaranteed to produce success. Planning for success may mean modifying standards so that a happy outcome is possible. In the family meeting, parents give some attention to planning learning experiences within the family that enable the child to develop a positive self-concept. For example, you can help the child select the tasks he wants to do and will be able to do well, thus giving regular opportunities to demonstrate competency and success. While a child can learn from the natural consequences of a mistake, it is equally important to plan successes that will create for him an image of self-confidence.

SKILLS OF ENCOURAGEMENT

Encouragement is not only a philosophy and a value statement; it is based on a set of *skills*. Without skills parents may be enthusiastic, may want to be more positive or encouraging, but are inept because they have not understood it requires specific skills. The following are some of the basic skills of encouragement:

1. Focusing on assets, strengths, and resources. When you are an encourager, you begin by identifying a person's assets. Too often in a relationship we tend to look for the individual's limitations and weaknesses. There is an assumption that the relationship will be improved by pointing out the child's weakness, as if this would bring an immediate correction. On the contrary, it tends to bring withdrawal, rejection, and resistance.

Even when you have identified liabilities in your child, you need to consider how that liability can be turned into an asset.

To be skilled at focusing on assets, you need to be an explorer who discovers hidden resources. Often, just beneath the surface of the talents your child is revealing are some additional resources that could be developed. As you patiently look for them, you will then have an opportunity to focus on strengths and the individual.

2.   Perceptual alternative skills. The person who has developed perceptual alternative skills has the ability to consider a variety of ways to interpret a specific event. For example, the child comes home with a low grade. You now have some alternative ways you can respond: by pointing out the weaknesses on the report card or by listening to how your child feels about it and ways in which he has decided to deal with the problem.

Parents who are able to work effectively with perceptual alternatives can always see something positive in any given situation. You can actually turn the situation around and make it more acceptable by focusing on even the smallest possible potential. When you feel comfortable with perceptual alternatives, you can deal with each challenge fully aware that there is a solution. You can then see a variety of possibilities and are less discouraged.

3.   Humor skills. Humor helps you to be aware that almost everything can be seen and understood differently. It provides you with the ability to develop perceptual alternatives, to shift your perspective from the negative to the positive, from anger to merely being upset. Humor skills give you the ability to modify your perceptual and emotional response. Humor frees you from discouragement, depression, rejection, and the negative emotions that accompany the discouraged outlook on life.

It is important in developing humor to be able to see yourself in perspective or to laugh at yourself, to accept your own imperfections and mistakes. Reducing your own self-constricting approach modifies your limited point of view and gives you far more options.

4.   Focusing on efforts. This is in contrast to those who focus only on completed actions or outstanding behaviors. For example, your child brings home a test paper with four right and sixteen wrong answers. The teacher marked the test "failure." However, you have a choice of how you will respond. You can emphasize the sixteen wrong, or you can focus on the four that are right, thereby showing a more spontaneous, creative behavior, which produces the opportunity to increase the child's self-esteem and motivation. You may point out something about those problems that were done particularly well or indicate some potential.

When you focus on an effort, you can take a unique approach to the situation. You will not be limited by all the negative concerns that some people have when they are evaluating another person. Instead, you will become alert to any strengths or assets, any positive movement. You will focus clearly on the effort, not on the final process.

DIFFERENTIATING PRAISE AND ENCOURAGEMENT

Often encouragement is confused with praise and reward. While praise may be of value, it can also be discouraging if the child maintains a low opinion of himself or becomes dependent on an external reward. Praise is like a reward for something well done and implies a spirit of competition. The unspoken message is clear: "Only if you do well will you be recognized." Praise may make members of the group who do not receive it unwilling to try. The child who sees a sibling praised while he is ignored is often permanently discouraged in that particular area.

John, eleven, and Gary, ten, were returning from their tennis lesson.
MOTHER: Gary, you really hit the ball exceptionally well today. I am very proud of you.
GARY: But my backhand wasn't very good.
MOTHER: It was much better than last week. John, didn't Gary do well?

This type of exchange, in which there is clearly praise for Gary and none for John, may cause John to abandon his efforts in tennis. It also sets Gary up for failure and discouragement if he does not continue to be outstanding. Praise is based on external evaluation and must be continually earned. Although the child enjoys receiving praise, he is never sure when he will get it again. In addition, he may come to expect it and thereby fail to function when it does not occur.

In contrast to praise, encouragement may be given for any effort or for slight improvement. And while praise may make the child feel special, encouragement is not concerned with superior-inferior relationships but focuses on helping the child feel worthy. The benefits of encouragement are long-range but lasting. Self-confidence and self-respect give the child the courage to accept the challenges life offers.

THE LANGUAGE OF ENCOURAGEMENT

Our autocratic tradition, emphasizing punishment and reward, has trained us to prod and nag rather than encourage. Often our language merely echoes the comments our own parents made to us. We must learn new words and phrases if we are to be effective in changing the child's view of him- or herself.

However, encouraging language cannot hide a negative basic attitude, for the child is readily able to detect insincerity and pretense. If the parent sincerely values the child just because he is human, with both potential and liabilities, encouragement will flow freely. This approach to parent-child relationships brings joy to the parent as well as to the child.

Focus your conversation on recognition of effort rather than on accomplishment. This places a value on the child as he is, not as he could be. This type of communication will stimulate the child's capacity to see the positive, and eventually it will influence his own vocabulary and communication processes.

The contrast between encouragement and words that discourage and do not foster growth can be exemplified as follows:

WORDS THAT ENCOURAGE	WORDS THAT DISCOURAGE
Knowing you, I'm sure you will do fine.	Knowing you, I think you should do more.
You can make it.	You usually make mistakes, so be careful.
I have faith in you.	I doubt that you can do it.
Thanks for your help.	If you had finished clearing the table, that would have been helpful.
You're doing fine.	You can do better.
I enjoyed that song.	Your music is getting better, but you missed the notes at the end.
I can see you put a lot of effort into that.	That's a good job, but the corners are ragged.
You have really improved.	Well, you're playing a little better than last year.
You'll figure it out.	You'd better get some help; that looks very difficult.
You can only learn by trying.	I doubt you should try.
That was a good effort; don't worry about the mistake.	Why didn't you think of that before you started?
Let's think this through together.	How can you be so dumb?
You've done some good thinking. Are you ready to start?	That plan will never work.
That's a challenge, but I'm sure you'll make it.	That's too difficult for you. I'll do it.

The difference between discouragement and encouragement is often very subtle, for it is affected by the perceptions and the courage of the child. For example, in a good relationship the child can perceive the parent's intent as positive even though his words may be critical and appear to be discouraging.

DETERRENTS TO ENCOURAGEMENT

The challenge to build an encouraging relationship with the child is an awesome one, particularly to those of us who were raised in the autocratic tradition, which placed an overemphasis on excellence and being superior. This orientation has influenced us to consider deficiency and failure to comply as violations of the demands and obligations of society. The democratic approach to human relationships does not expect more of a child than can be produced.

We must recognize that by tradition we are better equipped to find fault, humiliate, and demand. Faultfinding and humiliating behaviors occur most typically when we feel that our status and prestige are threatened. We are most inclined to discourage when we feel that the child is spoiling our self-image. As adults, we must look at our own competitive relationships with people within our family and community. Do you feel that your child must be a product that makes you look good? Are you overconcerned with being the best parent? In order to see the child's assets, you must build a new, optimistic relationship based on your courage to be imperfect and satisfaction with your progress as a parent. Our children will not develop the courage to be imperfect unless they have examples to emulate.

THE COURAGE TO BE IMPERFECT

Our success with children often depends on our own standards and expectations. We have suggested that children need to be encouraged and that they should not be involved in pursuing perfection. It is only consistent to suggest that we are not interested in developing the "perfect parent." In reading this book, you will recognize that there are many situations in which you as a parent will continue to have difficulties. No one can master all of the ideas. You cannot change your feelings and your behavior to the extent that you no longer have relationship problems with your child. The illusion that one can become the perfect parent must be dispelled. We might even go further and suggest that even if you could become such a paragon of virtue, it would not be good for the child. Perfect relationships at home would leave him unprepared to deal with all the faulty relationships in the real world.

If the parent is going to provide a model for human relationships, he must have a sense of his own personal strength and worth. He must not view his every mistake as a failure. In contrast, he must be able to see his own progress and not be pessimistic if changes do not occur immediately.

The courageous parent will not believe that the child's mistakes and faulty behavior are a personal attack or an insult to his strength or prestige. He will come to recognize that even though he has a most sincere commitment to a new approach and expends great effort, he will not be able to overcome all of the difficulties with the child. But it is essential that the parent have the courage to deal with his own imperfections and the desire to change old habits. This courage serves as a catalyst for the development of new human relationships. The target is not perfection, then, but developing the ability to cope effectively with the challenges of parent-child relationships.

BEING MORE ACCEPTING OF YOURSELF

We have stressed the importance of accepting the child. But the child will not get this message unless the parent is able to accept himself. That is why we have also encouraged the parent to become more accepting of his own behavior. Many parents who feel extremely dissatisfied with their children are really, basically, dissatisfied with themselves. We are suggesting that the parent must become fulfilled as an adult so that he doesn't require that his child serve as a symbol of his success or a buffer for his frustrations. For many parents, their children have become symbols of their status in the community. Parents must not depend on the child to represent them and to elevate their self-esteem. He is a separate being with unique needs, goals, values, and attitudes. The parent should involve himself in work and recreational and social relationships that produce the satisfaction he may have formerly sought from producing the perfect child.

FEELING GUILTY

Many parents report that they feel very guilty about the way in which they deal with their children. They say, "I know I am not doing things right; I'm too lenient or not strict enough, and I feel very guilty." We would like to emphasize that feeling guilty is often a cover-up. It is a suggestion of good intentions that we do not really have. We often observe people who feel guilty about such things as smoking, drinking, and poor communication with their spouse but do nothing to improve or correct the situation. It is almost as if their expression of guilt makes them acceptable as good persons with good intentions regardless of the fact that they really do not intend to change.

Sometimes parents play games with themselves when they recognize that their relationship with their child is unsatisfactory. They believe that the open acknowledgment of their guilt is sufficient. Supposedly, their expressed good intentions should excuse their poor performance. But expressions of guilt do not solve the problem. If you want to change, make use of your capacity to decide and start to function in a more effective manner.

AVOIDING SELF-DEFEATING PATTERNS
OF BEHAVIOR

Parents are handicapped by a number of basic self-defeating patterns that are often the result of their faulty ideas about themselves and human relationships. We suggest that you look closely at some of the faulty assumptions that may cause a poor relationship with your child.[1]

1. It is necessary to be loved or approved of by everyone in the community.
2. One must be thoroughly competent in all aspects of child training if he is to be considered personally worthwhile.
3. It is catastrophic when things do not turn out the way one would like.
4. Disobedience is a personal challenge to one's strength as a good parent.
5. We can do little about our problems, and we are victims of circumstances.
6. The child's history determines his present behavior, and there is little that we can do to bring about a change.
7. The parent is completely responsible for the child's misbehavior, and since the child is only a product of the relationship, the child would not misbehave if the parent were a more effective person.

All of these mistaken ideas produce poor human relationships. They make the parent feel that he is "not okay." The parent must first change his beliefs, perceptions, actions, and attitudes before he can develop new relationships. These self-defeating patterns do not have to be repeated. The parent must choose to change.

AVOIDING DISCOURAGEMENT — BEING POSITIVE

Throughout the book we emphasize the debilitating effects of discouragement on the child and caution the parent to have courage. As he develops his own personal philosophy of child training and examines his faulty assumptions about human relationships, he will recognize that he can change his own behavior and hence his relationship with the child. He can begin by making small but definite, positive steps. He must accept his efforts and not feel guilty about, or discouraged by, his mistakes. We suggest that the parent regularly assess the positive qualities his child possesses. In addition, the parent should do this for himself. When he begins to get discouraged, he should focus on his accomplishments rather than on his failures.

The parent who is person centered is aware of the child's feelings as well as his own. He shows his love and affection spontaneously, and at unexpected moments, and through physical contact, he may communicate: "I really think you're wonderful." He does not wait for the child to produce and then acknowledge that "the B on the report card is very good." A person-oriented parent is skilled at recognizing strengths and assets, and he is encouraging to the child.

4

MAD, SAD, GLAD . . .
UNDERSTANDING EMOTIONS

>-+-•->--0--<•-+-<

Billy gets a new toy, and he's happy. Bobby takes the toy away, and Billy is angry. They fight over the toy and break it, and Billy is sad. Billy goes to his mother seeking sympathy, and he may find her angry with him for destroying the toy.

E MOTIONS INVOLVE THE feeling life of the individual. And while it seems as if emotional responses are automatic, they are actually learned. You can decide how you will respond. Your beliefs create emotions and behavior. Choose new beliefs and you will have new feelings. Choice influences your emotional state.

Emotions are an important part of every transaction between parent and child. However, because parents are often not attentive listeners, they may not hear the feeling. In other instances they choose to ignore the feeling and may even tell the child to forget the feeling. In this manner we deny the child the growth of his emotions. Without awareness of their own feelings, children cannot become sensitive to others.

Emotions can be a positive force that serves to energize and enrich experience; they can create a feeling of belonging. They can be a source of strength and motivation or disorient, disrupt, and create social alienation. Whatever we learn has an emotional component, that is, joy, anger, enthusiasm, fear. Emotions give life its color, richness, energy, and completeness. They are a part of all our experiences. We "love" to play a sport, or we "hate" to practice our music. Our emotions have a powerful influence on our behavior and attitudes and affect how we perceive a situation. In some instances joy and sympathy bring us together with people; feelings of anger and sadness may cause a separation. Since each child will experience the full range of pleasant and unpleasant feelings, the parent needs to help the child understand and become comfortable with feelings. When families provide acceptance, love, and respect, they support emotional development and growth. Recognition, enhanced self-esteem, and the stimulation of courage and self-confidence are the result of emotionally healthy families.

PURPOSIVE EMOTIONS

Emotions are sometimes viewed as forces totally beyond our control. We say, "I'm so angry I can't think," or "I was so afraid I forgot." It is important that parents understand and recognize that emotions are purposive, helping a child attain a goal. Emotions generally support the intentions of the individual and provide energy and motivation in line with the goal. Emotions, beliefs, values, and goals are interrelated. When you understand that the child's emotions are patterned, meaningful, and interrelated, you will be less confused than if you view the factors as separate entities.

> The grandparents are visiting, and during a shopping trip Tom, four years old, wants a car in the toy section of the store. His mom indicates that he already has many cars like it and they cannot buy another one. Tom starts to pout and cry. The grandparents are sympathetic. They

intercede and say they will buy the car for Tom. Tom has learned that emotions in the form of water power serve a purpose: They help him get his way.

It is time for Joan, six, to go to bed, but she complains that she is not ready. Getting no response except a firm "Get going now," she resorts to crying. Dad, moved by her tears, agrees to accompany Joan to her room and read her a story. She becomes special and earns attention and service through the use of emotions.

During incidents with emotional overtones the parent can ask, "What does my child expect to have happen by being so emotional? What does he expect me to do?" Awareness of the social context in which the emotion occurs (the specific interaction between parent and child) helps the parent understand the goal-directed nature of emotions, and the parent becomes aware of the way in which the child chooses a certain emotion to provoke a specific response.

Feelings are always present, and the parent can become more skillful in recognizing their potential value. It is not desirable or healthy to teach the child to deny feelings even if they are negative. Emotions are capable of generating genuine and positive involvement as well as forcing others to cooperate or give in to our demands.

GOALS EMOTIONS MAY ACHIEVE

Parents can recognize how emotions can serve purposes and intentions by noting characteristic situations in which purposive emotions may be employed:

1. Emotions may be used to get *special attention*. When a child is especially sad or temperamental, he may receive special treatment and sympathy. The emotion enables him to get the extra service and attention he would not obtain in another way.

Jim has lost his football, and the game has to stop. The boys decide to go to another field where Sam has a ball. Since Jim doesn't own the new ball, he can't make the rules or conditions for play. But Jim is accustomed to making the rules, and now he is not willing to go along with the rules Sam has made. At home Jim complains about the other children. His parents console him, and although Mom is very busy, she feels compelled to make a special trip to replace the football. Because Jim is treated in a special way at home, he continues to try to get similar treatment from the other boys.

2.   Emotions may be used to *control*. The temper tantrum and displays of anger often bring power to the child and enable him or her to control the situation. This can occur at home or at school.

The teacher changes Jack's seat at school. He is moved from the front of the room and is therefore no longer the teacher's helper, nor does he get special attention. He becomes very angry and pouts and fusses until the teacher finally gives in and returns him to his former place.

3.   How does your child use emotions to control and get his way? Emotions can serve the purpose of *retaliation* for what is thought to be unfair treatment.

The boys are deciding on a game to play. Fred wants to play basketball, but the other boys choose baseball. Fred does not get his way. He becomes angry and starts to fight with John, who had persuaded the boys to play baseball. He feels it is fair to fight, since John opposed him.

4. Emotions can be used to *protect us from functioning*. When we are discouraged, we may use sorrow or weakness to get support and special service.

> Sally gets very "nervous" whenever Mom asks her to practice her spelling. She becomes confused, incoherent, and whimpers. Mom feels sorry for Sally and indicates that she does not have to practice spelling. Sally has learned how to use her feelings to escape expectations.

Emotions are of positive value when they elicit our concern or empathy for the feelings of others. The increased sensitivity improves social relationships. Even temper may have a value insofar as it is a way of helping the child stand up for his rights when he is defeated or frustrated. However, when temper (usually in the form of tantrums and demands) is used to control others, the self-centeredness impedes full emotional development.

How can the parent change the negative emotions that impede emotional maturity? The temper tantrum is an interesting example of behavior fueled by negative emotions. When the child is temperamental, the natural tendency is to show him that he can't get away with it. We become emotionally involved, trying to prove that we cannot be manipulated this way. Depending on the situation, the parent may attempt to control by shouting or threatening the child. If others are present and the parent is embarrassed, there may be an attempt to bribe the child to stop the temper display. Such a strategy only encourages or intensifies the tantrum. The child's sense of timing in regard to control is usually far superior to the parent's natural ability to help him grow emotionally. However, you need to learn to help the child understand and manage his or her feelings.

Since the temper tantrum is usually an emotional show, it requires an audience. The most effective procedure in dealing with a temper tantrum is to leave the child alone. When dealing with a temper tantrum, it is most important not to be intimidated because of the presence of friends, relatives, or strangers.

The child who displays temper tantrums will use a variety of methods to get his way, including stomping, screaming, crying, threatening, and begging. Whenever you attempt to subdue the child, the child will win, for you have reacted. If the child does not get attention, it is highly likely that the temper tantrum will end.

Temper tantrums are power plays designed to force a parent to give in to a child's demands. Whether you give in or become angry and punish the child, your reaction tends to reinforce the child's tantrum, which is "If I can't have my way, at least I can get you upset."

Eight-year-old Roger had a history of temper tantrums. When things did not go his way, he would scream, cry, and stamp his feet. Dad had tried everything, from ignoring him to pleading, reasoning, and spanking. Nothing would stop the tantrums.

In discussions with the counselor, Dad became aware that Roger knew how to get him upset. Whenever he didn't like a particular situation, he would punish Dad for it. The counselor suggested that when Roger gave his next performance, Dad should retire to his room, lock the door, turn up the radio, and read a magazine—or he might take a walk. He shouldn't reappear until Roger was finished with his tantrum.

Dad reported that it took several trips to his room before Roger began to realize that his tantrums were a wasted effort. Roger even tried screaming, pounding, and kicking the bedroom door. Dad didn't respond; he simply turned up his radio. After a short time Roger became much more peaceful.

In working with tantrums, it's important to have a very set plan. You can't "try" one procedure, then another. Instead, you have to follow through consistently with the procedure. Roger knew that his father could not succeed in his efforts to ignore him. All he had to do was increase the intensity and Dad would eventually react to his performance. However, when Dad removed himself and placed the door between himself and Roger, Dad was able to convince him that he was no longer impressed with his son's behavior.

FEAR AND ANXIETY

It is normal to anticipate that the young child may be fearful at times, afraid of loud and unexpected noises or of strangers. These types of fears can be crucial to the survival of the child. But fear and anxiety are often a product of personal perceptions in combination with creative imagination. One must distinguish between fears that may be reality based and those that are the product of biased perceptions or are created by the child for a specific purpose.

Children appear to be born relatively free of fear. But an adult's overanxious or oversolicitous behavior can help create the conditions that give rise to fear. If the parent is fearful and not sure the child will succeed, the child will almost always live up to that expectation. The child often operates with an awareness of the social consequences of behavior. For example, fearfulness may win the child special service or control over others. While there are situations that merit caution and an awareness of danger, protecting the child from certain harmless and valuable experiences only inhibits his emotional growth.

The child needs to develop courageous but reasonable approaches within the limitations involved in walking in traffic, using potentially hazardous tools, or playing with animals. There are a number of training procedures that can be used to teach a cautious approach to real danger. They involve developing and stimulating the child's intelligence, thereby enabling the child to distinguish between what is a valid opportunity or gamble and what is a foolish risk or chance.

When a child is fearful, she needs to have access to someone who is willing to listen and understand. Often the opportunity to ventilate in the presence of an empathic person is effective in coping with the fear. After the child has expressed her apprehensions, the parent can "reflect understanding" of what the child is experiencing. Once the child is aware of parental support, the parent and child together can explore ways to overcome the fear.

> BETH: I don't want to go into the pool.
> PARENT: It seems very dangerous to you.
> BETH: I might sink.
> PARENT: Since so many of your friends swim, would you like to play in the water, too?
> BETH: I'm not sure I could.
> PARENT: Let me help you by the side of the pool.

This approach is characterized by understanding and accepting the fear first and then helping the child to reduce her fear. Never laugh at fear; to the child it is very real and threatening.

In other instances fear may purposefully be used to control adults. Avoid preaching, blaming, manipulating, bribing, cajoling, and begging. Refrain from becoming involved in excessive talk. If the parent is unimpressed by fears but supportive of the child, the purpose for being fearful will be eliminated.

Mr. and Mrs. Zersky's six-year-old daughter, Brenda, was afraid of sleeping by herself in her room. Both parents had repeatedly reassured her that there was nothing to be afraid of. Despite their efforts, Brenda continued to be afraid. She cried, screamed, and often fled to her parents' bedroom for comfort. On many other nights her mother would have to go to Brenda's room and stay until she fell asleep.

One night Mr. and Mrs. Zersky decided to try a different approach. They told Brenda that they felt she was a big girl and capable of sleeping by herself. They informed her that the door to their bedroom would be locked and that they would not come to the door or go to her room.

Later that evening they heard Brenda whining. Although Mrs. Zersky was tempted to go to the door, she refrained from doing so. In a few minutes Brenda began screaming and pounding on the door, complaining that she was afraid and pleading with her mother to please accompany her to her room. Mother made no response. After several minutes of screaming, Brenda began to quiet down and eventually became silent.

In the morning Mr. and Mrs. Zersky found Brenda sleeping on the floor outside their door.

The next night, Brenda tried again to get her mother to pay attention to her fears. Again she was unsuccessful. After that, Brenda stopped trying to get her mother to come into her room.

The fear of rejection is one of the special fears with which children often need help. A child often gets most of his status from belonging and being accepted. When his position is dependent on approval, he may be afraid to make a mistake. This type of fearful approach is best corrected by helping the child see that his parents accept him as he is.

Susie was an outstanding fourth-grade student and received much praise for her schoolwork. The class was now beginning some new math processes that she was not able to master immediately. Her mother noticed that instead of the usual eager presentation of her math papers, there appeared to be no math papers at all. While cleaning Susie's room, she found a paper with many mistakes and a note from the math teacher: "This work is not up to your standards." Susie's exaggeration of the danger of mistakes and her fear that she was no longer acceptable to her parents had led her to hide the paper.

The next afternoon, Susie's mother asked how things

were going in math. Susie began to cry and told how difficult it had become. Her mother's acceptance of her feelings and her assurance that she understood enabled Susie to bring out the papers, seek assistance, and begin to realize that she could learn from her mistakes.

The fear of the dark may be genuine or purposive. Accept the fear and listen to and understand the reason behind it. Experiences in which the child gradually controls the dark through the use of lights help him learn to control this fear.

Joe, five years old, was afraid of the dark and insisted that one of his parents stay in his room with him until he fell asleep. As soon as they started to slip out after a time, he called and fussed, which served to hold the parents captive.

JOE: *Don't go. It's too dark.*
DAD: *When there is no light, you're frightened.*
JOE: *It's very scary.*
DAD: *I'm going to put a lamp in your room. That way you can turn it out yourself when you're sleepy, or I'll turn it off when I go to bed.*

The fear of school is frequently related to a fear of separation from parents. It is also a way of controlling the parents by eliciting sympathy.

Bonnie refused to attend school. Whenever it was time to go, she would dawdle, have a temper tantrum, or pretend she was ill. These methods usually immobilized her parents. Either they became involved in a power struggle, or they gave up. After seeking professional advice, they tried a new approach. They indicated to Bonnie an understanding of her feelings, encouraged her to express her fear, and explored ways to deal with it, but they firmly insisted she go to school.

MOTHER: It's time for school.
BONNIE: I can't go. I'm sick.
MOTHER: You don't feel well?
BONNIE: My stomach hurts, and I feel very weak.
MOTHER: You are afraid something might happen at school.
BONNIE: I don't like the kids, and the teacher is mean to me. They are all very mean. I hate them and school. I won't go.
MOTHER: I know you're very angry and scared. Do you want to walk to the car by yourself, or do you want me to help you get to the car?
BONNIE: I won't.

Mother took Bonnie's "I won't" as her decision to be helped to the car. She firmly took hold of her hand and escorted her to the car.

While it is important to listen to Bonnie's feelings, it is equally important to provide a firm but kind approach.

Fear of school often indicates a lack of independence. Does the child get special attention, a sense of winning, or receive pity? Does the child cause his parents discomfort? The fear is often complicated by parents who feel inadequate because they should be able to get their child to go to school but cannot. The accompanying social embarrassment the parents experience tends to reinforce the behavior. Professional consultation may be necessary if the situation persists.

PROMOTING EMOTIONAL GROWTH

Emotional maturity is always relative. A child may be very mature in his feelings about work and responsibilities and at the same time be quite immature in terms of relationships with other children. Emotional maturity fluctuates because emotional development is not steady and continuous. Similarly, emotional flexibility and capacity to cope may vary from day to day and from situation to situation. The child becomes able to conquer a fear in one area while acquiring anxious feelings in another. For example, he may be able to accept defeat in games while becoming despondent about a single mistake on a school paper.

Adults as well as children continually work toward the integration of beliefs, feelings, attitudes, and actions. As we are permitted to be open, honest, and free to relate our feelings, we become more sensitive to self and others. We cannot expect emotional growth to proceed like physical growth; it is not constant but is subject to moving forward as well as slowing down. But as parents permit the child to become independent and self-sufficient, he begins to accept responsibility for his behavior, and emotional maturity is facilitated and promoted.

CONDITIONS FOR EMOTIONAL GROWTH

Emotional growth proceeds best under the following conditions:

1.   In a democratic climate whose egalitarian premise is concerned with equal rights and responsibilities. The democratic atmosphere provides freedom that is naturally accompanied by responsibility. The child learns from the social and natural order that although she is free to play with friends, do work, or tease an older brother, she must be prepared to accept the responsibilities and consequences that follow from this choice.

2.   When the climate encourages open expression of feelings, whether negative or positive. It is not only permissible but expected that one express real feelings. When parents try to change feelings by denial and repression, they encourage holding emotions in, which eventually produces depression, anger, and rebellion.

Because the parent has lived longer does not entitle him or her to ignore what the child is saying and feeling. Even more important than understanding the content of the child's message is recognizing the feelings that underlie it. The parent must listen for the emotions that the child expresses and respond empathetically; empathy is essential in stimulating emotional growth.

As the parent becomes more attuned to the child's language and becomes a more experienced listener, she can help the child become aware of the intentions, purposes, and goals behind his emotions. Then, as the child becomes more aware, the parent can begin to discuss with the child better ways to reach his goals by participating in the give-and-take of life.

3. When the child is ready for a new experience. This readiness includes physical, social, and motivational factors. Avoid pushing the child into physical or mental activities in which you have ambitions for the child; the child may not yet have the coordination, social confidence, or interest to provide the necessary foundation for success.

4. When the child develops a vocabulary of feeling words, that is, sad, angry, upset, scared, worried, etc. In talking with the child, identify her feelings and communicate what you have observed. "You are angry. You seem upset. Could it be you're worried?" Encourage the child to identify your feelings and to express what it is they are observing. Helping the child become aware of her feelings and teaching the child to express what it is she is feeling help produce emotional growth.

5. When the parent-child relationship is neither overprotective nor oversolicitous. It must involve mutual respect and an atmosphere in which the child is encouraged to join in new experiences and is allowed to learn from them.

Gary comes home enthusiastic about joining the Little League, and his mother immediately thinks of the additional demands on herself for driving, supervision, and attendance at games. She has a job that keeps her late at

the office several days a week; it could interfere with getting Gary to the games. She is also aware of the pressures involved in competitive baseball. But despite her
hesitations, this is a time for Gary's mother to avoid being overprotective and encourage her son to get involved
in a new learning experience.

6. For the very young child who shows interest in a new skill
or hobby, the parents can consider making learning experiences
available that will ensure some success. Encouraging positive efforts and avoiding comparing the child to more experienced children will allow the child to take small but positive steps.

COMPETITION

The capacity to be competitive has value when it enables an individual to move toward self-initiated goals. Self-competition
that helps the individual play music more beautifully or improve
skills and become a more productive member of a team are examples of measuring your own progress and social development
instead of comparing yourself with others. However, while we
want children to excel, we must be careful not to misuse competition.

The overly competitive child is frequently one whose parents set standards that are too high or blame the child for failures. In those cases the child loses his self-confidence
altogether or harbors the false belief that real worth depends on
being first or a winner. The child believes that any loss or failure
will diminish his or her self-esteem and value. Consequently,
the child retreats from all competition, thinking it is better not
to try at all than to do so and possibly fail. The youngest child in
a family of exceptional athletes may decide not to play sports
because his belief is "I cannot live up to the standards of my
predecessors."

Competition and bribery should never be used to motivate.
The child who is very competitive feels his or her ability is never

enough; always needing to achieve more results in overambition. The child strives for more than can possibly be accomplished, and distorted standards leave the child continually dissatisfied and discouraged. Constant striving to be better and failing is a sign of overambition. Parents can help the child understand and accept occasional failure as a fact of life by publicly acknowledging the parents' own mistakes without complaining or moralizing.

Parents often expect their child to compete in areas in which the parents are competent. The child may perceive that the parents expect outstanding results in school or athletics, for example. If the child believes he can't meet the parents' expectations, he may either compensate in other areas or offer inadequacy as an excuse for not competing. It is important to avoid transferring your personal goals of achievement to your child.

Accept and value what the child is doing instead of evaluating it. We do not grade and hold our friends to standards. If we did, we would lose them! The child benefits more from being valued than evaluated. While the parent may accept the child's feelings of uncertainty and fear of failure as realistic, the parent assures the child of her worth and acceptance regardless of achievements. It is important for the child to come to feel that a good effort alone makes her worthwhile. Be more concerned with attitudes and the courage to try than with meeting high expectations. The courageous child learns to set goals that are realistic. Maturity involves developing standards that are internalized and personally satisfying.

DEALING WITH DISCOURAGEMENT

The child who feels inadequate or defeated manifests discouragement: "I can't satisfy myself or others." A discouraged child may use emotions to avoid facing the tasks of life.

When dealing with the discouraged child, it is important to deemphasize external standards. Let the child know that you accept her direction of movement and encourage attempts and efforts. Let the child know that mistakes help us learn.

Susie was painting a picture. She hesitatingly looked at the range of colors and then asked her dad for a suggestion. Dad declined to comment and only smiled.

SUSIE: Should I take the yellow or orange?
DAD: You don't know which color to choose?
SUSIE: What will be the best?
DAD: It's your picture, and whatever you like will be fine.
SUSIE: What do you want?
DAD: I know you would like me to choose for you, but I like your ideas.
SUSIE (pointing to yellow): Will yellow be okay?
DAD: Whatever you decide will be fine.

DEALING WITH FEELINGS

Often when your child is expressing feelings you may wish to be someplace else. Your first instinct is to stop the flow of feelings. Instead, begin by acknowledging those feelings. Listen closely to what your child is expressing. Let the child know you care about what he or she says by expressing the feeling the child has shared. "It seems . . ." "It sounds like . . ." "You feel . . ." Don't deny or attempt to repress the feelings. In dealing with them, begin by being aware of your own feelings of annoyance, anger, or despair. Use this awareness to tune into what you and the child are feeling. Then respond by expressing those feelings. Don't ignore them; doing so is a way of telling the child that they don't count. Remember, what your child perceives *is truth* for the child. Since you are not in the child's place, how can you be sure you are right and she is wrong?[1]

To be effective in redirecting a child's goals, adults need to alter their behavior and their feelings. Parents need to learn to stop feeling annoyance, anger, hurt, or despair as a first response to misbehavior. Parents learn new behavior so that they can respond, instead of merely react, to the child's behavior. But changing their feelings may be very difficult.

Emotions are purposive and provide the energy to move a person to action. Mosak[2] points out that both Adler and Ellis believe that "emotions are actually a form of thinking, that people control their emotions through controlling their thinking."

BELIEFS AND GOALS ASSOCIATED WITH ADULT RESPONSES TO THE FOUR GOALS[3]

Goal 1.   Inappropriate bid for attention. Adults may feel annoyed and believe "I have a right to continue what I'm doing without interruption," which is true. However, the second part of the belief, "You should stop interrupting me," produces difficulty in the relationship. It contains a demand that the child will challenge. Adults need to focus not on reinforcing the child's misbehavior but on looking for attendant behavior so that the child becomes self-reliant.

Goal 2.   When a child pursues power, adults may feel angry if they see this as a threat to their prestige and authority. If adults decide to fight the child to prove who is boss, the anger will serve the purpose of establishing control. If adults decide not to fight or give in, they will win the child's cooperation.

Goal 3.   Vengeful behavior is difficult to handle because adults may believe that the child does not love them. Adults may generate hurt feelings to give themselves permission to get even with the child.

Once the adults recognize that the attack comes from the child's own deep discouragement, they will be in a position to develop different beliefs. You will find yourself experiencing regret and empathy for the child's hurt. Then you can concentrate on improving the relationship.

Goal 4.   A feeling of despair is experienced when a child displays inadequacy. The adult's feelings are generated to grant the adult permission to give up and disown any responsibility for helping the child. To counteract these feelings of inadequacy, adults must first develop feelings of faith and confidence and convey them to the child.

Rudolf Dreikurs, a prominent psychiatrist and recognized authority on human behavior, advocated changing emotional responses and beliefs.

1.   Avoid your first impulse and do the unexpected. Dreikurs indicated that your tone of voice is the best indicator of attitude and feelings.[4] If adults deliberately concentrate on offering choices with a friendly but firm tone, they will not feel annoyed or angry. In addition to the tone of voice, attend to the nonverbal "toner," such as facial expression, gestures, and body posture, as these are also indicators of attitudes and feelings.

2.   Divert yourself. Force yourself to focus on another thought or activity. Focus on a pleasant scene, television, reading, shopping, hobby, anything that diverts your thoughts.

Plan a specific time to feel annoyed, angry, etc. Choose a time of day when the child is not present and spend five minutes talking out loud about what you are experiencing regarding the child's behavior.

3.   Dispute the belief that creates the emotions. Recognize the purpose of the emotion you want to change and then search for the sentences you need to tell yourself to create the emotion. Aggressively attack the negative beliefs by silently taking charge of your thoughts.

Think of a frequent problem with a child. Explore the results of continuing to have a negative belief and the more beneficial atmosphere produced by changing to a positive one.

The following steps are repeated three times at each sitting and are essential to the process:

a. The adults imagine themselves in a frequently occurring scene with a child that invites them to feel and act negatively.
b. They then locate and say the usual negative belief to themselves and experience the resulting feelings.
c. Next, the adults begin to think of all the ultimate negative consequences that can occur if they continue to believe their disjunctive beliefs and emote and behave in line with the beliefs. For example: "If I continue to believe I have to get even with Dave, I will continue to become hurt and angry and punish him. He will probably continue to rebel and get even. Our relationship will probably deteriorate even more. I won't enjoy him. He may do something to intensify his retaliation, such as stealing or using drugs." The adults continue to list the negative consequences for about a minute, then stop and repeat the entire process two more times during each period. It is important to encourage adults to fantasize the worst possible results of continuing to believe those negative beliefs that lead to negative emotions and behaviors.[5]

4. Develop reminders and signals that will alert you to appropriate responses. A note on the mirror such as "Watch your tone of voice" will remind you how to communicate. Posting cartoons may illustrate your reminder.

All these ideas will help you develop a sense of humor about otherwise serious situations. Experiment with the procedures that "work" for you. If you want to learn more about managing your emotions in all aspects of your life, read:

How You Feel Is Up to You: The Power of Emotional Choice by Gary D. McKay and Don Dinkmeyer (San Luis Obispo, Calif.: Impact, 1994).

5

IS ANYBODY LISTENING? . . .
COMMUNICATING WITH CHILDREN

*JULIE: You never listen to me. You don't care how
I feel!
DAD: That's just about enough from you. Get to
your homework!*

*RICH (crying): Tommy got mad and said he didn't
want to play with me anymore. Then he and the
other guys told me to go home.
MOTHER: That's too bad, honey, but don't worry,
you'll find some other friends.*

*DAD: You get in here right now. Just look at this
mess. I leave you alone for one minute and look
what you do!*

*MOTHER: You're late again! When I tell you to be
home by ten, you'd better be home by then or else!*

Maybe this sounds familiar. As parents, most of us weren't
trained to listen to our children—or other adults. We may not
know what to do when children share their feelings. We also

may not know how to communicate our feelings effectively to our children—or each other.

Perhaps the most essential skill for successful human relationships is communication. If we study people who are successful in life, we generally find effective communicators. They know how to listen to others and how to communicate their own ideas and feelings in nonthreatening ways. They're generally accepting and understanding of the feelings of others.

Watch an effective teacher as she patiently listens and accepts the ideas and feelings of her students. In turn, when she talks, they listen. She's usually successful in influencing them.

Unfortunately, most parents are poor communicators when they deal with their children. They correct, nag, and punish to no avail. In order to influence their children, parents need to learn how to accept, listen, clarify, understand, and express their own feelings. They must become effective communicators.

ROLES WE PLAY THAT SHUT DOWN THE LINES OF COMMUNICATION

Parents often respond in discouraging ways when children express their feelings. These responses alienate the kids and reflect the following negative roles:

1. *The commander in chief* (ordering, commanding, threatening, controlling):
   "Now, listen here, don't you talk to me like that!"
   "I said, get busy!"
   "Do it—or else!"
   "You're going to do what *I* say."
2. *The moralist* (preaching, patronizing):
   "That's not the right thing to do."
   "You shouldn't do things like that."
   "Good little boys don't do those things."
3. *The know-it-all* (lecturing, advising, reasoning, appealing to the child's logic, being superior):

"That just doesn't make any sense."

"If I were you I would . . ."

"Now, you know better than that."

"I've had much more experience than you and . . ."

4. *The judge* (making pronouncements, evaluating):

"You asked for it."

"You didn't do your best."

"Well, if you'd studied harder . . ."

5. *The critic* (ridiculing, name-calling, sarcastic, joking):

"You're just lazy, that's all."

"You think you're a big shot around here."

"Ah, come on now, she can't be that bad. I imagine being in a classroom all day with a bunch of little monsters
like you would drive anyone crazy!"

6. *The psychologist* (diagnosing, analyzing, probing, inter-
rogating):

"Your problem is . . ."

"How long have you been worried about this?"

"Okay, tell me exactly what happened."

7. *The consoler* (reassuring):

"Everything is going to be all right."

"All children feel that way at times."

"Don't worry, it's just a stage you're going through; you'll
get over it."

When children get these kinds of responses, they often feel
defensive, misunderstood, or resentful; more than likely, they'll
stop sharing their feelings. We miss many opportunities to help
children handle their feelings and to build a good relationship
when we rely on such responses.

RESPONSES THAT KEEP LINES
OF COMMUNICATION OPEN

Basic to effective communication is acceptance. Many times
lines of communication are severed because individuals, partic-

ularly children, avoid expressing their true feelings and thoughts for fear of rejection.

Parents have traditionally believed that the way to influence a child is to refuse to accept her. This is a false assumption. Because the child so deeply desires acceptance, she'll go to great lengths to try to justify her behavior. When the parent insists that her attitude is wrong, the child will think of ways to defend it. But if the parent can accept her feelings and help the child express them, the parent may open the way to a consideration of other alternatives. The child will feel comfortable and understood, and now that she has rid herself of her burden, she can begin to think clearly and explore other methods of meeting her needs more satisfactorily.

It isn't enough for the parent to feel accepting toward his child. He needs to express that acceptance. A simple indication by the parent that the child is understood can be sufficient. For example: "I see," "I understand," "I know what you mean." It's also helpful for the parent to engage in more specific feedback concerning what he thinks the child is feeling.

Acceptance is frequently communicated through nonverbal clues, such as facial expressions, posture, or gestures. A smile and a pat on the back need no accompanying words, for they signify acceptance. Likewise, a scowl or disapproving glare speaks volumes as well.

When you avoid interfering in an activity in which the child is engaged, you also demonstrate acceptance. For example, if the child is building a model airplane and you don't offer assistance unless he asks for it, you will indirectly communicate to him that his efforts and methods of attacking the project are accepted. Don't be concerned about whether the child is approaching the problem correctly. Instead, allow him to make his own mistakes and set his own standards. The child's sense of accomplishment and satisfaction are what is most important, not the procedure or the product. Interfering in order to show the child the "right" way often conveys nonacceptance by indicating to the child: "You're not capable."

Nonverbal acceptance may simply involve listening. When

you let the child talk freely, you indicate by your accompanying nonverbal behavior, such as expressions and posture, that you're interested, accepting, and attempting to understand what she is trying to communicate. You indicate by your silence that you genuinely want her to share her feelings.

LISTENING SKILLS FOR PARENTS

There are several ways you can respond more encouragingly to your child's messages. The "tell me" technique and the "contact" technique are means of eliciting feelings and demonstrating acceptance and understanding at the same time. The "tell me" technique helps you demonstrate that you're willing to "tune in" to the child's verbal and nonverbal clues.

> *"Sue, you sound as if you're really upset. Want to tell me about it?"*

> *"John, you look as though you're quite worried about something. Would you like to tell me?"*

When tuning in, it's best to aim for deep feelings. This way the child can easily modify your interpretation. Whereas if you don't go deep enough, she may think you don't understand and will no longer feel inclined to express herself.

The contact technique conveys attentiveness, understanding, and acceptance. You maintain contact with the child while he's revealing his concerns and anxieties. The contact technique basically has two dimensions: recognition and reflection. The recognition dimension, utilizing responses such as "I see," "Oh?," "I understand," "Yes," "I see what you mean," indicates to the child that the parent recognizes her feelings.

Reflection is a more specific aspect of the contact technique. It involves clarifying and rephrasing the child's feelings. Children don't always use feeling words to describe their feelings.

So you often have to "decode" the words the child uses, and reflect what you think the child is feeling.

> *TIM: That Johnny is a real jerk!*
> *MOTHER: You're really angry with Johnny.*

The child's words are not the true message, they're merely his own way of communicating his feelings. Reflection serves as a means of checking whether you understand what the child is feeling. If you don't, your child will tell you, and you can try again. Reflection also provides a mirror for the child to see himself clearly. The child becomes aware of the picture he projects to others. As in television instant playbacks, the child is able to see and understand the impression he creates. After the feedback is received, your child can decide whether he likes the image or wants to change it. Such mirroring is called "reflective listening."

Sometimes the child will use emotional or "feeling" words to communicate her feelings. When this happens, choose a synonym for the word the child uses.

> *KAREN: I just hate Carl. He embarrassed me in front of the whole class!*
> *DAD: You're very angry with Carl, and you're afraid of what the other kids will think.*

By choosing synonyms for the child's feeling words, you'll avoid parroting—just repeating the words you hear. Instead, you'll be making a sincere attempt to understand, in your own words, what the child is feeling.[1]

Sometimes when children are upset they won't say anything, but you'll know by a look or by posture that something's wrong. Tune into these nonverbal clues.[2]

> *"You look sad, want to tell me about it?"*
> *"Something's bothering you, want to talk about it?"*

Reflective listening takes practice. To help you in your attempt to decode and mirror your children's messages we've developed a feeling vocabulary. Below is a list of feeling words and phrases that you can use to provide feedback.

POSITIVE FEELINGS	NEGATIVE FEELINGS
Happy	Unhappy, sad, upset
Glad	Sad
Proud	Ashamed
Satisfied	Dissatisfied, disappointed, disgusted
Everything's working out according to plans	Feeling as if nothing's going right
Sure, certain, determined	Confused, worried, puzzled, doubtful
Fair	Unfair, cheated, feel like getting even, picked on
Warmth, warm	Distance, distant
Respected	Worthless, put down
Feeling good about self	Not happy with self, stupid, jealous
Accepted	Rejected, left out
Courageous, brave	Fearful, afraid
Secure, confident	Insecure, uncertain, lacking faith
Comfortable	Uncomfortable, mad, angry, annoyed, irritated, hurt
Trusted	Distrusted, accused
Aggressive	Shy
Important	Insignificant, small
Excited	Bored
Honest	Dishonest
Encouraged	Discouraged, defeated, feeling like giving up, guilty
Sympathetic	Indifferent
Dependable	Can't be counted on
Independent	Dependent
Ambitious	Lazy
Patient	Impatient
Like, love	Dislike, hate
Responsible	Irresponsible

When your child sends a feeling message, you can use the feeling vocabulary to reflect. It's especially important to acknowledge the depth of the feeling by using words like "very," "really," "pretty," "awful."

> *KEITH: That Johnny is a real jerk!*
> *MOTHER: You're really angry with Johnny.*
> *KEITH (crying): He broke my model.*
> *MOTHER: You feel very sad about that.*
> *KEITH: One of these days I'm gonna break something of his.*
> *MOTHER: You're angry and want to get even.*
> *KEITH: I sure do.*
> *MOTHER: You want to hurt him as he's hurt you.*
> *KEITH: Yeah!*

> *MARY: Dad, look at this model I built.*
> *DAD: You're really proud of it.*
> *MARY: And I did it all by myself.*
> *DAD: Looks like you feel pretty good about being able to do it yourself.*

It's important not to approach the feeling vocabulary list mechanically. If you're merely saying words but not conveying your understanding of the feeling, then the child won't feel understood and may think you're not sincere. Reflective listening is effective when it's done in the spirit of mutual respect and with an honest attempt to understand.

Make the tone of your reflective-listening responses tentative; you can't know for sure exactly how your child is feeling. You're making your best guess.[3] When you give a declarative response such as *"You feel sad . . . ,"* you're in effect telling the child how she feels. By using a tentative tone, "You feel sad . . . ," you're simply checking out a hunch.

A complete reflective-listening response involves stating the *feeling* and the *situation* that prompted the feeling.[4] For example, "You're happy because . . ." "You're upset about . . ."

"You feel hurt because Martin canceled your date."

"You're bored because it's raining and you can't play outside."

"You're excited about your part in the play."

A simple formula can assist you in constructing a reflective-listening response: "You feel . . . because . . ." In some of our examples, you'll notice that we don't always include the word "feel." Sometimes you just need to state the feeling. "You're disgusted with the whole situation." And we don't always use the word "because" to relate the feeling to the situation that prompted it. Use whatever phrasing is more natural to you—as long as you pick up the feeling and the situation involved.

"That's a tough situation. Sounds like you're worried about it."

"Looks like this is going to be very challenging, and maybe you're concerned about how you'll handle it."

You may want to begin with the more formal "You feel . . . because . . ." until you get used to reflecting feelings.

Generally it's best to take time to listen whenever the child wants to talk; open communication and mutual caring require nourishment. But occasionally you may not have time to finish listening to all the feelings your child wants to express. Rather than leave the child before he has finished, sending him the message that you don't care, it's best to arrange an appropriate time to discuss the problem.

> GREG: *That teacher is so unreal! She's going to make all of us do detention tomorrow just because three kids were talking!*
> MOTHER: *You seem really angry about this, Greg, and I'd like to listen to you, but I've got an appointment in a few minutes. Can we talk about this when I come home?*

In many cases the child may not reach her own solution during the listening session. Although it's difficult for parents to resist offering suggestions in an attempt to "set her straight," advice will block communication. The child won't feel understood or trusted enough to make her own decisions. Many times, having rid herself of the burden of unpleasant feelings, the child will find alternatives on her own after she's shared her feelings with you. Your purpose at this point is just to listen, understand, clarify, and feed back.

If the child can figure out her own solutions, fine, but there will be times when she needs more help. In these situations, you can use a process called "exploring alternatives." (Chapter 6 will discuss this process.) For now, let's turn our attention to how you can effectively communicate your feelings to your children.

GETTING CHILDREN TO LISTEN TO YOU

So far we've discussed how to listen and respond to your children's feelings. But how do you express your feelings so that you're understood and respected?

Unfortunately, when most parents want to tell their children something, they play the same roles they assume when listening—the commander in chief, the moralist, and so on. Talking to the children in these ways creates "parent deafness." They tune you out. Children don't want to hear advice, threats, ready-made solutions, reasons, warnings, or a review of their faults.

The difference between ineffective and effective communication can be seen simply by thinking in terms of "you-messages" and "I-messages."[5] Most messages sent by parents contain the word "you": "You'd better not do that." "You know better than that." "You'd better stop that." "Don't you think you should . . . ?"

If the parent simply tells the child what she's experiencing when the child acts a certain way, the message is usually an I-message. "I can't read when someone is making noise." "I'm worried that I will be late if I have to wait much longer." "I want to take a nap, and the noise is keeping me awake." "I don't like seeing socks and shoes all over the family-room floor because I work hard to keep the house straightened up." An I-message focuses on the parent rather than on the child. Instead of blaming the child, the parent shares his or her experience.

I-messages are generally more effective because, unlike the you-messages, they don't convey disrespect and criticism and are less likely to produce antagonism and resistance. They place the responsibility for finding a solution on the child. Her behavior is producing unpleasant consequences for the parent, therefore, it's the child's job to decide what to do about it. I-messages convey trust in the child to find appropriate solutions. In addition, the honesty of I-messages often influences the child to send honest messages in return.

There are generally three parts to an I-message:

1.   A nonevaluative description of the behavior: "When I find your bicycle in the driveway . . ."
2.   The parent's feeling about the consequences the child's behavior has for the parent: "I feel disrespected."
3.   Indication of how the consequences of the child's behavior specifically interfere with the parent: " . . . because I have to get out of the car and move it."

A simple formula can assist you in forming I-messages: "When [such and such happens] I feel [state your feeling] because [state the consequences your child's behavior has for you]."

You've discussed—with your teen—rinsing dishes as they're used and placing them in the dishwasher instead of letting them pile up in the sink. He ignores the discussion.

"When I find dishes piled in the sink instead of rinsed and put in the dishwasher, I feel discouraged because I have to stop and clean up the sink before I can fix dinner."

Your five-year-old daughter and her friend are chasing each other through the house.

"When I see Jenny and you running in the house, I get scared because someone could get hurt or something could get broken."

Your eleven-year-old son calls you a name.
"When I'm talked to like that, I feel disrespected because it puts me down."

Of course, you can vary the formula: "I feel disrespected when I'm talked to like that because it puts me down." It's very important to tie your feelings to the *consequences* the child's behavior has for you—emphasize the *because*. In this way the child is more likely to see that it's the result of his behavior that's troubling you rather than the behavior itself—or the child as a person. Besides, there may be circumstances when the same behavior wouldn't bother you. For example, if it's your teenager's night to cook and he leaves dishes piled in the sink, he has to deal with the dishes; it's his problem now.

Whenever possible, keep the word "you" out of your I-message. Saying "you" can be interpreted as blaming the child. Use phrases such as "When I see," "When I find," "When I hear." Of course, there are times when you can't avoid saying "you," but use it as infrequently as you can.

You can use the feeling vocabulary developed for reflective listening to help you identify your feelings.

Avoiding Hostile I-Messages

In using I-messages your tone of voice is crucial. If the I-message contains tones of hostility, it will have the effect of a you-message, for hostility is an emotion that is aimed at another person. The focus isn't on the speaker but on the person spoken to. It's best to identify the source of the hostility. Usually it traces back to an initial feeling that wasn't shared.

The Blacks invited their old friends the Kellers to play bridge. The evening before bridge night the Blacks discussed their concern for Mr. Keller's drinking problem and what they should serve during the evening. They finally concluded that they'd put all the liquor away and say that Mr. Black's doctor had advised him not to drink for several months and therefore they simply didn't have anything in the house to serve. Mom and Dad were unaware that six-year-old Barry was listening very intently and digesting every bit of information.

The next evening, the Blacks proceeded according to their plan, but Mr. Keller foiled them by bringing along a bottle of bourbon as a gift. When Barry came in from playing and saw the drinks, he said, "It looks like Mr. Keller found that liquor you hid, Dad."

It's understandable that Barry's parents would be angry; however, if they decide to talk to Barry, they will probably be more successful if they identify the source of their anger as embarrassment and say something like "When you told Mr. Keller about hiding the liquor last night, we were embarrassed and afraid that we might lose a friend."

When you're feeling angry, ask yourself, "What did I feel before I got angry?" Usually there's another feeling associated with the anger. For example, if your five-year-old wanders off when you're in a large store, you might first feel frightened before you get angry. Identify the other feeling and express it. "When you wander off, I really get scared because something might happen to you."

Being Prepared to Listen

When you use I-messages, be prepared to listen reflectively, because the I-message creates a problem for the child. He has to decide what to do about your feelings.

Dad comes home from the store and discovers that twelve-year-old Ellen has had her friends in the house.
DAD: *When I come home and find that you've had other kids in the house when you agreed not to, I really feel let down.* [I-message]
ELLEN: *I'm old enough to look after things, Dad!*
DAD: *You're angry and think I don't trust you!*

[Reflective listening]

ELLEN: You don't!

DAD: I can see where you might feel that way, but I feel that I do trust you. If one of the other kids got hurt while I was away, I'd be held responsible, and I'd be pretty unhappy about that. [Respecting how the child feels and sending another "I-message"]

In many cases the child just wants to be heard; reflective listening helps him feel understood.

Verbalizing Your Positive Feelings

It's important to send I-messages about your positive feelings as well. Your child benefits from knowing that you feel good about her. Such messages help her feel that she's appreciated and loved. Remember to tell your children that you love them. Love is often taken for granted, but nothing feels better to a person than to be told that she's loved by someone she cares about. In addition to verbal statements about positive feelings, a smile, a hug, a kiss, all express genuine good feelings.

SOME FINAL COMMENTS
ABOUT COMMUNICATION

The "tell me," "contact" techniques, and reflective listening are skills you can use when your child owns a problem. I-messages help you when you own the problem. (For a discussion on problem ownership, see chapter 6.) These skills are effective in many cases, but there are some points to keep in mind:

- *Don't try to force your child to talk.* Sometimes when you reflect a feeling the child will deny the feeling or simply not want to talk about it. You can leave the door open: "If you want to talk about it later, I'll listen."

- *Realize that the responses that seem "unnatural" at first will become "natural" as you practice.* Reflective listening and I-messages are new ways to communicate with children. Like the other skills you're learning in this book, they'll seem foreign to you. But ask yourself, "Is my way of communicating now helping my children or me?" If the answer to the question is no, then it's time to learn this new language.

Also recognize that you don't have to be a perfect communicator. For example, if you miss a feeling your child's trying to express, she'll correct you. As long as you're making a sincere attempt to understand, your child will know you care.

- *Keep questions to a minimum.* Asking a lot of questions can lead the child to think he's being interrogated. Make a statement about what you're observing and hearing instead of asking a question. "How did you feel when that happened?" could be turned into a statement: "It sounds like you're feeling sad about that." Save the questions for times when it's really challenging to understand. "I'm having some trouble understanding how you're feeling. Could you tell me more about it?"
- *Don't overdo reflective listening.* You don't need to respond to every question or statement. "Where's the jelly?" doesn't need a reflective-listening response, "You seem to be longing for something sweet." It just needs an answer. As you tune into your child's communication, you'll learn the difference between questions that just need answers and those that indicate a need for discussion of feelings.
- *Don't give up if reflective listening doesn't produce immediate results.* This is new to your children, too. It may take them time to realize that you just want to understand.
- *Keep children's goals of misbehavior in mind.* Sometimes reflective listening can reinforce a child's goal of attention. If your child comes to you with the same or similar problem over and over, she may be more interested in having

your undivided attention than in solving the problem. If this happens, you can tell the child that it seems you're unable to help her with the problem or that it looks as if it is something she'll have to work out for herself. If she keeps trying to come to you with the problem, keep silent and focus your attention on something else. Your child will learn that you're there to help when she really wants help. Give her attention at unexpected times by focusing on something positive.

If you think your child is expressing feelings to gain power over you or to try to get even, you may decide just to listen or to withdraw from the conflict. See what works best for you.

I-messages are often unexpected responses and don't reinforce negative goals like you-messages. But there are exceptions to this. If you find that your child is seeking your attention and begins to expect you to state your feelings, you may find ignoring the misbehavior or applying a logical consequence more effective. (See chapter 8.)

In some cases, I-messages can stimulate power contests or reinforce revenge-seeking behavior. If this happens, it's best to discontinue their use and discuss the problem at another time, when you and your child aren't in conflict.

Your experience with these skills—and others that you're learning—will tell you which ones are the most effective for you. Give each skill you're learning a full effort; don't expect immediate results.

6

TALKING IT OVER: SOLVING
PROBLEMS AND MAKING DECISIONS

IN CHAPTER 5 you learned about reflective listening and I-messages, two skills to help you improve communication with your children. Good communication can solve many problems, but what do you do when it doesn't? In this chapter we'll discuss another skill, exploring alternatives, a skill you can use to solve problems with your children.

Before you can decide what to do about a particular problem, you have to determine whose problem it is and who's responsible for solving it. We call this problem ownership, or Who owns the problem?

WHO OWNS THE PROBLEM?

Reflective listening is one skill you can use when your child has a problem. I-messages can help you when you experience a problem with your child's behavior. In order to recognize when to use these methods, you need to become familiar with the concept of problem ownership, or Whose problem is this?

In parent-child relationships, ownership is best determined

by thinking in terms of whose desires or rights are interfered with.

1. The child has a problem because he is thwarted in satisfying a desire. It is not a problem for the parent because the child's behavior in no tangible way interferes with the parent's rights (and the child's safety is not an issue). Therefore, the *child* owns the problem.

2. The child is satisfying her own desires (she is not thwarted), and her behavior is not interfering with the parent's rights. (There are also no safety issues.) Therefore, there is *no problem* in the relationship.

3. The child is satisfying his own desires. (He is not thwarted.) But his behavior is a problem for the parent because it is interfering in some tangible way with the parent's rights (or the child's safety is involved). Now the *parent* owns the problem.[1]

Some examples of parent-owned problems could be how your teen uses the family car, curfews, safety issues, interruptions, failure of a child to do chores that impact on you, use of the telephone, running in the house, playing loud music, and misuse of family property.

Some examples of problems that could be owned by the child are uncertainty about career choice, feelings of inadequacy, rejection, loneliness, disappointment, frustration, anger, poor school performance, lack of discipline in school, difficulty with homework, conflicts with a brother or sister, and difficulty in getting along with peers. Of course, ownership of a problem depends on the child's age. A five-year-old can be expected to tie his own shoes; it's his problem. But a two-year-old would not be expected to have this skill; therefore, the parent owns the problem.

Unfortunately, many parents assume ownership of their child's problems and feel responsible for her behavior at school, with brothers and sisters, and with peers and neighbors. By assuming ownership of what should be the child's problems, the parent deprives his child of opportunities to learn how to handle problems effectively, hampers his relationship with the child, and decreases his influence. Reflective listening and exploring alternatives can help the child become responsible for solving her own problems.

When parents decide to "transfer ownership," that is, to allow the child to take responsibility for the problems he encounters in his life, they can help the child develop problem-solving abilities. Transferring ownership does not mean you no longer care about the child; rather, that you care enough to be concerned about the child's development. You can now accept the child, listen, and demonstrate concern and understanding, but you must always realize that the child is an individual separate from you who must work out his own problems.

Now that you have some understanding of problem ownership, let's look at another skill, exploring alternatives, which can help a child discover a solution to a problem she owns and can help you negotiate an agreement with a child when you own a problem. This skill is useful when your reflective listening and I-messages aren't sufficient.

EXPLORING ALTERNATIVES WHEN THE CHILD OWNS THE PROBLEM

While reflective listening is an effective tool for demonstrating acceptance and understanding as well as for strengthening the child's problem-solving ability, exploring alternatives is also a valuable way to help the child learn to cope with life's problems.

When you permit your child to choose and decide, you not only treat him with respect, you begin to allow him to be responsible for his own behavior. Allowing him to choose and believing in his ability to make a good decision are important communications. This type of faith builds courage.

The problem-solving approach, then, must elicit and help clarify the child's feelings and beliefs: "You are confused about what to do next; both possibilities are attractive."

It assists by summarizing: "It seems so far you've said . . ."

If there is a block to progress, the parent may pose her ideas in a tentative form: "Is it possible that because . . . ?"

Or you may encourage the child to look at the problem more creatively: "While you don't know exactly why this is a problem, what would you guess is the reason?" . . . "Let's pretend this was happening to Tony. Why would it happen to him?"

In some instances, the parent can be most helpful by role reversal. Here the child takes the role of the person he is having a problem with and the parent plays the child's role. The parent models a different approach to the problem. Then they discuss how this approach can produce different results.

We recommend that you concentrate on developing your reflective-listening skills before you attempt to enter into exploring alternatives. If you move too quickly into this phase, the children may misinterpret your motives as the old methods in a new disguise. However, when the relationship is good, then both you and the child can enter this phase with all your resources (beliefs, feelings, and experiences), and together you can explore uncharted territory. There is nothing that you're trying to obtain, win, or sell; your entire purpose is to help the child get in touch with her feelings and develop her critical thinking ability.

Sarah comes home crying.

> *MOTHER: You seem very upset, Sarah. Want to talk about it?* [Recognizing feelings and utilizing the "tell me" technique to encourage dialogue]
> *SARAH (crying): The kids at school are always picking on me.*
> *MOTHER: It must be frightening to go to school every day.* [Reflective listening]
> *SARAH: It sure is; no one likes me. They're always*

calling me names. I go out on the playground, and Joan says, "Here comes Stupid." Then the other kids start to call me Stupid.
MOTHER: *What do you do then?* [Beginning to explore the interactions to determine how Sarah unknowingly contributes to her problem]
SARAH: *I tell them they're stupid. Joan hits me, and we get into a fight.*
MOTHER: *How does it end?*
SARAH: *The teacher stops it and asks us what happened. I tell her about Joan and the others and she punishes them.*
MOTHER: *Does that end the problem?* [Clarifying the failure of Sarah's present method]
SARAH (*sighing*): *No, it happens over and over again.*
MOTHER: *Sounds as though you just don't know what to do.* [Reflective listening]
SARAH: *Yes.*
MOTHER: *Why do kids pick on other kids?*
SARAH: *Because they don't like them.*
MOTHER: *Why don't kids like other kids?*
SARAH: *I don't know.*
MOTHER: *What would be your guess?* [Encouraging exploration]
SARAH: (*shrugs her shoulders*)
MOTHER: *Is it possible that kids pick on others because they're fun to pick on?* [Posing a hypothesis]
SARAH: *What do you mean?*
MOTHER: *Well, they get mad or cry and tell the teacher.* [Clarifying]
SARAH (*reflecting for a moment*): *Yes, I guess you're right.*
MOTHER: *If that's true, then what else could you do when they call you a name?* [Encouraging exploring alternatives]
SARAH: *I guess I could ignore them.*

MOTHER: How could you do that? [Exploring Sarah's understanding of the concept of ignoring]

SARAH: Just walk away and not pay any attention to them.

MOTHER: Okay—but how would you feel inside? [Helping Sarah understand the full meaning of ignoring]

SARAH: I would probably feel mad.

MOTHER: Yes. And remember how we decided that they liked to get you angry. [Reviewing the purpose of the children's teasing]

SARAH: Yes.

MOTHER: If you decided not to get mad, do you think they might leave you alone? [Helping Sarah realize cause and effect]

SARAH: Maybe.

MOTHER: Walking away is one way to deal with the problem. Do you think there might be another way? [Summarizing and stimulating exploration of an additional alternative]

SARAH: What?

MOTHER: Why don't we act out the problem? You play Joan, and I'll play you. Okay? [Demonstrating a solution through role reversal]

SARAH: Okay.

MOTHER: You call me names.

SARAH: Here comes Stupid.

MOTHER: Yes, that's right, here I am. Old Stupid is back! [Illustrating the use of an unexpected response that disarms the teaser]

SARAH: (dumbfounded, unable to say anything)

MOTHER: What's the matter? Why did you stop? [Helping Sarah analyze the role-playing]

SARAH: I don't know.

MOTHER: Is it hard to tease someone who doesn't get upset and just agrees with you? [Posing a hypothesis]

SARAH: Yes.

MOTHER: *How do you feel about that way to handle it?* [Encouraging Sarah to express her opinion and any doubts about the alternative]

SARAH: *They would probably laugh at me.*

MOTHER: *That's true. What could you do then?* [Stimulating further problem-solving skills]

SARAH: *I guess I could just laugh with them.*

MOTHER: *Do you think they might stop eventually if they couldn't get you upset?* [Posing a hypothesis]

SARAH: *Yes, I think so.*

MOTHER: *How could you act toward them at other times, when they're not picking on you?* [Exploring a more total approach to the problem]

SARAH: *I could be friendly.*

MOTHER: *Let's see now; we've discovered two ways to handle the problem—ignoring and agreeing with them. I would suggest you choose one or the other and stick to it. Don't do both or they'll just wait to see what you'll do next. Do you want to try out one of these?* [Summarizing and pointing out the consequences of inconsistency, Mother leaves the final decision to Sarah. It is her responsibility to solve the problem. A commitment is sought]

SARAH: *Yes, I think I'll just agree with them.*

MOTHER: *Shall we talk about it again next Tuesday to see how it's going?* [Setting a time for evaluating the plan]

SARAH: *Okay.*

(They decide on a time.)

The Steps in Exploring Alternatives

As the example of Sarah illustrates, there are steps for exploring alternatives.[2]

1. Understanding and clarifying the problem. The "tell me" technique and reflective listening are helpful here in sorting out the feelings and beliefs.

2. Exploring alternatives through brainstorming. In this step, you help the child look at possible solutions. Brainstorming is an effective technique for exploring alternatives. You elicit as many ideas as you can from the child without judging. Delaying judgment encourages creativity. After all ideas are given is the time to evaluate with the child which ideas would work best. (See step 3.) If the child has difficulty coming up with ideas, you can make suggestions in a tentative way: "What do you think would happen if you . . . ?" or "Have you ever thought about . . . ?"

3. Evaluating ideas and choosing a solution. Here the child looks at the ideas that have been generated and decides which one she thinks will work best. If you see a problem in her choice of an approach, encourage her to think about the possible consequences of that choice. You can also give your opinion. "It seems to me that . . . What do you think?" But remember, the choice is the child's (dangerous situations excepted, of course).

4. Getting a commitment and setting a time to evaluate the plan. It's very important to get the child to commit to action. It's interesting to talk about possibilities, but nothing will happen unless the child acts. Watch out for phrases such as "I'll try." Trying and doing aren't the same. "I'll try" is a weak commitment; the child tries it once, it fails, and she gives up. Encourage the child to actually *do* the new behavior until a set time regardless of results. In this way the child can give the new behavior a fair test.

A time to evaluate results is very important. The child is encouraged to use the plan, not forever but for a specific period of time, such as a week (shorter with young children). When the time comes to discuss the results, leave it up to her to remember the appointment. If you remind her, she won't be taking responsibility for her problem. At the evaluation meeting, the child can decide to continue the plan or make another choice if it isn't working.

This is how you can explore alternatives for child-owned problems, but what do you do when you own the problem? We'll begin our discussion of this by taking a look at principles for conflict solving.

RESOLVING CONFLICTS

The spirit of cooperation is lacking in most homes. Both parents and children view conflicts only in win-lose terms. When conflicts are resolved on a win-lose basis, the loser—whether parent or child—usually resents being overpowered by the other, is unwilling to cooperate, and often seeks ways to retaliate. Few realize that there is a third way to resolve conflicts— the democratic way. Parents and children can stop fighting and work toward cooperation for mutual benefit. Rudolf Dreikurs and Loren Grey describe four essential principles for resolving conflicts democratically.[3]

1. Mutual respect. Each person must respect the rights of others. Without mutual respect there can be little willingness to cooperate.

2. Pinpointing the true issue. The issue at hand is rarely the true issue. The true issue is usually of a personal nature, such as prestige, winning and losing, unfair treatment, and rights. Conflicts with children always involve the child's mistaken goals: attention, power, revenge, or assumed inability. They also involve your goals of control, being right, or being superior: "I'm older, so I know what's best."

3. Reaching agreement. In any human interaction there is always agreement. In a conflict, the parent and the child have agreed to fight! However, when one person decides to stop fighting, the other can't continue the fight. Each person in a conflict usually thinks only about what his opponent should do. Instead, he needs to think of what he can do, thus making a new agreement possible.

4. Participation in decision making. Parents must involve children in the decisions that affect their lives if they wish to achieve cooperation. There must be full participation and shared responsibility.

Conflicts can be resolved democratically through natural and logical consequences. (See chapter 8 for a full discussion on consequences.) The parent removes herself from the position of authority, refusing to fight or give in. Instead, she allows the child to experience the results of his misbehavior and assume responsibility for his actions. The child has the option of deciding how he'll react to the situation.

Nine-year-old Richard and his new puppy were playing in the kitchen while Dad was trying to fix dinner.

Dad said, "I'm sorry, but I can't work with this going on. Would you choose to stop playing with the dog, or would you rather play with him outside or in your room?"

Richard replied that he'd play with the dog outside. However, in just a few minutes he resumed playing with the puppy in the kitchen.

Dad said, "I see you've decided not to play with the dog. We'll try again tomorrow."

Instead of becoming angry and ordering his son to leave the kitchen, Richard's father offered him a choice. Although Richard agreed to play outside, his behavior indicated that he had really chosen not to play with the dog at all. Father acted on his decision and assured Richard he'd have another chance.

Resolving Conflicts by Exploring Alternatives

Some conflict situations require discussion and the exploration of solutions that will be acceptable to everyone involved. But at the time when the conflict occurs, it's generally best to withdraw. If both the parent and child are quite emotionally involved, any attempt to discuss the issue may degenerate into a power struggle. It's generally best to postpone discussion of the conflict until a time when tempers have cooled, and there is a better chance to reach an agreement.

During the discussion of the conflict situation parents can use their reflective-listening skills as well as send their own I-messages. Begin the problem-solving session by stating the problem in a friendly, nonjudgmental manner. Tell how you feel and demonstrate that you understand the children's feelings. Then brainstorm solutions. Initially refrain from evaluating the suggestions. When the children finish, add your own ideas to the list, if needed. Then go over the suggestions one at a time until you reach an agreement.

The same steps for exploring alternatives when the child owns the problem apply to resolving conflicts when you own the problem. The difference is that you have a stake in the solution.

If the problem just involves one child, it's appropriate to explore alternatives with her individually. If the problem involves all the children, the family meeting is the appropriate forum. (See chapter 7 for a discussion of family meetings.)

Here's an example of exploring alternatives for a conflict with one child:

Joy is a single parent with one son, Don, fifteen years old. One Saturday night, Don comes home at 1:00 A.M. Joy is worried and angry. She chooses not to confront Don at this time and delays discussion until Sunday.

JOY: *I want to talk with you. When you came in at one A.M., I was very worried that something might*

have happened to you. [Clarifying the problem with an I-message]
DON: Ah, Mom, I can take care of myself! Besides, Dad lets me stay out late!
JOY: You sound annoyed because I brought this up. [Don uses the old ploy of trying to get Mom in an argument about what's appropriate at Dad's and at her house; she doesn't bite, but reflects his feelings instead]
DON: Well, no, it's just that I think I'm old enough to stay out late.
JOY: I agree, but I think one is a bit too late.
DON: Why?
JOY: Because bad things can happen late at night.
DON: Like what?
JOY: You know, crime, drive-by shootings . . .
DON: Ah, Mom. They can happen earlier, too!
JOY: I know, but I can't keep you under lock and key. One o'clock's just too late for me to feel comfortable. [Restating her feelings in an I-message]
DON: What time do you think I should be home?
JOY: What time do you think would be reasonable? [Joy involves Don in exploring alternatives by asking him for a suggestion]
DON: Midnight.
JOY: Okay, you think midnight. I would feel more comfortable with ten. [Joy adds her idea to the brainstorming]
DON: Mom!
JOY: We have two ideas, ten and midnight. How can we compromise? [Exploring alternatives]
DON: I don't know . . . maybe go in the middle?
JOY: You mean eleven?
DON: Yeah . . . but what do I do if the guys want to stay out later? I mean, they're gonna think I'm a kid!

> *JOY: You're worried about your reputation.*
> [Reflective listening]
> *DON: Yeah.*
> *JOY: Okay, suppose we agree on eleven. What could you say to the guys?* [Encouraging Don to come up with an idea]
> *DON: I don't know . . . you got any ideas?*
> *JOY: Well . . . you could blame it on me, you know, say you have a paranoid mother? (They both laugh.)*
> *DON: They'd just say that's your problem!*
> *JOY: True, but I still want to feel secure about this.* [Returning to an I-message]
> *DON: Mom, what if we agree that I'll be home by eleven or I'll call?*
> *JOY: That's an idea. I'm willing to go along with that to see how it goes.* [Making an agreement]

Don and Joy agree that Don will be home by eleven or he'll call. They agree to discuss it the following Sunday to see how it went. If Don violates the agreement, Joy may have to set limits. If he's not home by eleven or doesn't call, then he can't go out the next time. Also, if she finds Don continually avoiding the curfew by calling, she may have to set limits.

Sometimes limits are built into the agreement. For example, Don and Joy could agree that if he doesn't call, he can't go out the next time. Joy must agree to limits on her behavior as well. For example, no reminding or nagging. Remember that rules are for parents, too. You can't expect children to follow the rules if you don't.

SOME FINAL COMMENTS ABOUT TALKING WITH CHILDREN

In this chapter we've focused on how to help children solve the problems they own and what to do when you own the problem.

Now we want to discuss two additional communication concepts: listening to children's ideas and restricting talking to friendly conversation.

Listen: Children Have Good Ideas

Adults almost universally believe that they have all the solutions to daily problems. The parent fails to solicit and listen to his child's ideas, for, after all, he, the parent, is more experienced and therefore knows what's best. But children often do have good ideas, and listening to them with a receptive mind is a necessary ingredient in any satisfactory parent-child relationship.

> The family had acquired a new puppy. Dad was attempting to paper-train the dog. Whenever he caught the pup after be had made a mess on the floor, he'd scold him and place him on the paper.
> One day, nine-year-old Jim saw Dad disciplining the dog.
>
> *JIM: Dad, maybe if we watch him right after he eats, we'll catch him about to go. Then we could put him on the paper, and after he finishes, we could tell him that he was a good dog and give him a puppy biscuit. Maybe then he'd learn.*
> *DAD: You know, that sounds as if it might work. Let's try it.*

Jim and his dad made an agreement to take turns watching the pup. It wasn't long before the pup learned what was expected of him. Both Dad and Jim were pleased with their accomplishment.

Restrict Talking to Friendly Conversation

Curbing criticism and restricting talking to friendly conversation often improve family relationships. Tone of voice often indicates how one values the person he's talking to. Many failures in talking with children can be attributed to a harsh or condescending tone. Even when you're discussing problems with children, you can still remain friendly and respectful as well as firm. State your feelings in nonthreatening ways with I-messages, use your reflective-listening skills, and engage the children in problem solving.

Realize that your nonverbal behavior reveals your intentions as well as your words. As the late Rudolf Dreikurs said, many parents "shout with their mouths shut!" In other words, parents decide to stop talking about the child's misbehavior or to change their way of talking, but they continue to feel annoyed and angry. Your feelings are transmitted to the child through nonverbal clues, such as a frown, tight lips, narrow eyes, harsh manner, and smoldering silence. The child's perception is uncanny. Interviews with children have demonstrated that even though a parent may be in another part of the house, the children still know how the parent feels about their behavior.

7

PULLING TOGETHER: HOLDING
FAMILY MEETINGS

⊷•⊶•⊙•⊷•⊶

Aᴿᴱ ʏᴏᴜʀ ᴄʜɪʟᴅʀᴇɴ ꜰᴜʟʟ participants in your family? Are your children treated as equals, and do they have responsibilities as well as privileges? Do your children help plan chores and times to do them? Do you decide their recreational activities, study hours, and clothing? Do you treat your children less considerately than you do your friends?

We believe that having a voice in family affairs promotes responsible behavior and self-discipline. Children are allowed to participate in decisions that affect their lives. To develop a new and democratic relationship in the family, you will need:

1. The time and opportunity to communicate your ideas.
2. Feedback and reactions from the members of the family.
3. A commitment to invest time in communicating with children and processing feedback on a regular basis.

You need to decide on the type of relationships you hope to promote in your family. These relationships are dependent on the model established by the leadership roles of the parents.

Leadership roles can be classified as authoritarian, permissive, or democratic in style. These styles differ in terms of basic ideas.

While parents are seldom completely democratic or completely autocratic, it is possible to note the prevailing characteristic leadership style. In the past, autocrats were fairly successful, if we accept control as a criterion for success. The general abandonment of the autocratic model in politics, society, and education has caused the autocrat to be less effective in the family, more often humored or pitied than obeyed.

The original reaction to the autocratic style was the permissive approach, which avoids decisions and rules and does not lead to effective relationships. We have observed that when a child is raised only with self-interest, he soon becomes bored and unhappy. (For more information on autocratic, permissive, and democratic parenting, see chapter 2.)

The democratic approach has as its target the development of autonomous but interdependent individuals who are free to make choices in a socially responsible manner. The parent benefits from sharing ideas, receiving feedback, and delegating responsibility and engenders more cooperation while meeting less resistance.

The family meeting is one of the most effective procedures for instituting democratic procedures. It provides a regular opportunity for family members to communicate and listen to each other. New approaches and ideas can only be absorbed when they can be heard and discussed and when their relevance to specific situations is made clear. Establishing family meetings is a decision made by members of the family, usually parents. It is decided that in order to communicate more effectively, it is necessary to meet regularly to discuss relationships, share ideas, and make plans.

Productive family meetings are not motivated by a desire to control through a new gimmick, nor are they convened primarily to establish control and set rules. They are motivated by the desire to improve relationships, share responsibilities, and truly enjoy each other as members of a family. Family meetings allow each member to hear the others' feelings, beliefs, and values and to point out what is right and find assets instead of focusing on weaknesses. The meetings can provide a unique setting that may reveal positive as well as negative feelings and where children learn to listen to each other and parents have an opportunity to hear their children's perception of their needs and place in the family.

The family meeting is not a magical solution to human relationships; it can only be as effective as the good intentions and listening skills of the participants. But it provides a special opportunity to restore the human relationships within the family that the pace of modern living, television, and the mobile society have taken from us.

PURPOSE OF MEETINGS

The family meeting is a regularly scheduled weekly meeting of all members of the family, planned for a mutually convenient time when all can attend. If certain family members choose not to attend, decisions still can be made that affect them. If they desire to change these decisions, it is their responsibility to appear at the next meeting. The purposes of family meetings are to:

1. Create a feeling of belonging, mutual respect, and acceptance.
2. Improve open, honest communication.
3. Develop plans and agreed-upon decisions that make for cooperation and cohesiveness.
4. Resolve conflict.
5. Stimulate and increase the social interest in the family so that the level of cooperation is increased.

The meeting takes into consideration all of the relationships and business affecting the family. Typical family meetings include:

1. Opportunities to give information about coming events, plans for fun or work, changes in living arrangements or vacations: Family meetings might announce a weekend trip, the visit of a relative or special friend, the building or remodeling of housing facilities, and the implications of these events for living in the home. Progress by family members or progress on family concerns can be communicated. For example, members may announce progress made academically, athletically, musically, in clubs, or in neighborhood activities. The family meeting is a time for sharing good news and for mutual encouragement.

2. Plans and decisions: Children learn best when given the opportunity to plan, decide, and take responsibility for their judgments. The parent will secure cooperation most readily by allowing the children to participate in decision making that affects them directly. Dialogue, discussion, and varied opinions and ideas are always more time consuming, but plans and decisions are more satisfactory when they result from group thinking, increased involvement, and the cooperation of all family members. Participation in decision making also helps develop self-assurance in children.

3. An opportunity to deal with recurring problems that cause conflict: In contrast to times of conflict, when family members are primarily concerned with winning and venting their emotions, the meeting provides a chance to review the problem with perspective in a setting that is less crisis oriented. While members may still have a big investment in winning or getting their way, the emotional tone will be lower than in the midst of conflicts, which will permit better relationships and more creative thinking. Also, the intervening time between meetings often allows them to consider how others feel about the issue. Problems are not solved by anger, nagging, condemning, or avoidance but through dialogue that enables members to reach agreement.

4. An opportunity to discuss ways in which all may work together for the family good: In every family there is a variety of necessary tasks to be done involving food preparation, setting and clearing the table, washing dishes, disposing of garbage, cleaning the house, and running errands. The parent often takes on all these responsibilities, depriving the children of the opportunity to learn skills, contribute to the family, and become independent. Children and parents discuss the most effective way to share responsibilities, make decisions, and cooperate in accomplishing the tasks.

5. An opportunity to articulate concerns and complaints: Family living, by nature of its interrelationships and the proximity of members, produces tensions and disagreements. Poor communication and failure to state dissatisfactions with relationships, expectations, and responsibilities can provide daily conflict and irritation. At family meetings, parents and children can come together to express their feelings and make known things they would like to change.

Betty is always expected to wash dishes, but she would really like to get involved in the cooking instead. Dad feels that Betty resists helping. The opportunity to clarify produces understanding, more effective help, and most important of all, a relationship clearly signifying that Dad understands that there is a better way to cooperate.

Discussing differences of opinion at the weekly meeting can often eliminate continual bickering. If Grant and Rob have come to an agreement about television that Grant refuses to live up to, there does not have to be a daily argument. If they are not yet responsible enough to keep their agreements, television can be discontinued until the next meeting. Complaints can sometimes be deferred for more effective action by requesting that they be brought up at the family meeting.

6. A social learning experience: The family is the original source of attitudes toward social living. The child develops an opinion of self and social relationships in this setting. If our goal is to produce independent as well as interdependent humans who care about others, a good way to accomplish this is through interaction during the meeting. The child develops social interest, cooperation, and the capacity to give and take, while the parents and the entire family reap the benefit of improved relationships.

The meetings also help create feelings of involvement in the family, conveying an attitude that the child's opinion is of value. The child feels accepted and develops a feeling of belonging, which strengthens self-esteem.

INITIATING THE FAMILY MEETING

Meetings should begin only after the parents have a clear understanding of the purpose of the meeting. Moreover, they should foresee the benefits and have already decided to develop democratic human relationships.

In a family with two parents, it's best if both want a family meeting. If not, the meeting can also be conducted successfully by one parent if he or she believes in its philosophy and benefits. Even in situations where there is one parent and one child, it has been found that the regular opportunity for dialogue and discussion is beneficial and age is no handicap as long as the child can communicate clearly.

Once the parents understand the philosophy and procedures of the family meeting, they meet with the children to explain the format of the meeting. The children are involved from the start by participating in decisions about the time of the meeting and the place. It is important to select a time when all members can attend and to avoid times when fatigue or pressures of appointments will handicap progress and jeopardize the relationships. The family meeting is an essential element of effective family functioning and is scheduled in order to make the above happen. Some important points about family meetings:

1. Recognize and listen to all ideas. None is less important.
2. Value the person as well as the ideas.
3. Plan a simple activity (a trip to the park or library; a visit with a relative).

GENERAL RULES

The chairperson of the first meeting is a member of the family who is most interested in developing democratic relationships and who is able to hear feelings, identify beliefs, and help members see each other's point of view. Reaching agreement is a goal. The first chairperson is usually a parent, but each week the chair may rotate to another member of the family, perhaps passing to the other parent for the second meeting and then from the oldest to the youngest child, finally returning to the original chairperson. Even when children are considered incapable of leading, they may learn from the leadership example set in the first meetings. Only members of the immediate family attend the family meeting. Someone who lives with the family and is regularly involved with family business can be eligible for attending family meetings.

The chairperson's duties involve beginning and closing the meeting precisely at the prearranged times. It's best if the meeting usually lasts between thirty minutes and an hour at the maximum. If meetings are too long for the attention span of the ages of the children, they will lose interest. The chairperson decides who "has the floor" and keeps order so that each speaker can be heard. The chairperson helps the group focus on the topic at hand and does not accept a change of topics until there has been an opportunity for full discussion and some resolution of the concern.

Keep the rules for the family meeting simple. The purpose is to expedite communication between members, not to teach formal meeting procedures. The following simple guidelines should be sufficient:

1. A member may have the floor by being recognized by the chairperson.

2. When a person has the floor and is presenting ideas, members cannot talk.

3. It is a good practice to have other members of the family restate what was presented to improve listening skills.

4. Members who have the floor are asked to comment on the points or issue being discussed. The family is not to proceed to a new topic unless the issue being discussed is resolved or progress has been made.

5. Family decisions can be made that influence members who choose not to attend. Attending members, however, don't plot to punish those not attending.

6. Calling an emergency meeting or canceling a meeting requires the unanimous permission of all family members.

7. The goal of the meeting is communication and agreement on issues, policies, and relationships. When agreement cannot be reached, voting can be used as long as there is no attempt to impose the will of the majority on the minority and members have agreed in advance to settle deadlocks in this manner. It is usually best to reach decisions by consensus to avoid having a competitive, win/lose spirit invade the meetings. The purpose of the meetings is to teach how to compromise and reach agreement, not how to prove who is right or get your way.

8. Keep minutes in several places, such as the children's rooms and the kitchen, depending on family preference.

Rules can be arranged to fit special needs of the family.

One of the purposes of the meeting is the distribution of tasks and chores. The distribution is best accomplished by having both parents, and children, compile a list of jobs around the house: cooking, setting the table, clearing the table, disposing of garbage, errands, dusting, vacuuming, washing, ironing, shopping, care of pets, repairs, outdoor jobs, washing the car, care of personal belongings, care of one's own room, etc. After the list has been completed, the children can participate in deciding what services they would like to offer. It is important to avoid assigning children jobs that no one else will accept. Be certain their participation is a real contribution. If there are some unpopular jobs, such as taking out the garbage, all take turns performing the task.

The children can also participate in deciding on a fair way to distribute the jobs. Try to elicit volunteers. You can volunteer yourself for the less desirable jobs. This will help create a spirit of goodwill and a feeling of equality. Some families have resolved the issue by having a job jar containing slips of paper describing all the tasks for the week and when they are to be accomplished. The family members then pick slips from the jar. Each member accepts the job described on the slip selected. Each week a new drawing is held.

PROCEDURES AND THE FIRST MEETING

Choose an area where each member of the family can be comfortable. Encourage each person who lives in the house, including grandparents, for example, to join the meeting. The chairperson will open the meeting, and the assigned or volunteer secretary will record the minutes. The agenda might include:

1. Beginning with the second meeting, reading of the minutes of the last meeting. This will be essentially a report on decisions previously made.

2. Old business. Discussion of issues not resolved or situations that members may feel need to be changed.

3. New business. This usually includes plans for some pleasant undertaking by the family.

4. Paying of allowances or settling other financial transactions between parents and children.

5. A summary of the major points and decisions; clarifying commitments. Time for the next meeting is agreed upon.

The meeting is characterized by a spirit of mutual respect and a concern for open discussion and honest dialogue, with an emphasis on resolution of conflict through democratic procedures. When agreements made in the meeting are broken, the person(s) responsible for failure to cooperate will experience logical consequences. All agreements are in effect until the next meeting, at which time they can be renegotiated if necessary.

Since chores and allowances are two concerns usually regulated by the family meeting, we have chosen to present them in our sample family meeting, with further specific suggestions following.

EXAMPLE OF AN INITIAL FAMILY MEETING

This family consists of four members: Mom, Dad, Rob, eleven, and Ralph, nine.

> *DAD: I thought we might start having regular meetings where we could talk about how we feel*

about the way things are going in our family. If we have any problems, we could discuss them and make some decisions. What do you all think about this idea? Would you be willing to give this a try? (Family agrees to try.)

DAD: *Good. First of all, I would like to ask if this time and place are convenient for everybody.*

ROB: *The time is okay, but I don't like sitting at this table.*

DAD: *How do the others feel?*

RALPH: *I agree with Rob.*

MOM: *This is fine with me, but if the rest of the family is not comfortable, I would be willing to move.*

DAD: *Then we'll move. Any suggestions?*

RALPH: *Why don't we go into the family room? It's comfortable in there.*

DAD: *Is that okay with everybody? (Family agrees; after moving, Dad continues.)I have written down three things: (1) old business; (2) new business; and (3) distributing allowances. Under the old and new business we can talk about our complaints and problems and work to reach some agreements and solutions that are acceptable to all of us. Also under new business we could plan some family fun each week. How does that sound? (Family responds favorably.)*

MOM: *I guess first we might talk about rotating who leads the family meeting. (Family decides the order of the chairperson.)*

DAD: *Okay, now that we have that settled, maybe we can discuss the ground rules. Mother, will you take the minutes this time? (Family agrees, and Dad tells family about members speaking one at a time, listening to each other, etc.)*

DAD: *Do we have any old business, any problems*

or complaints about the way things are going?
ROB: *There are a lot of things I don't like. For instance, I don't like the job of taking the trash cans out and bringing them in. When both cars are in the garage, I'm afraid I'll scratch one of them. And it's too smelly and grubby. The puppy's papers are the sloppiest job of all.*
DAD: *In other words, you don't like to do unpleasant jobs.*
ROB: *That's right.*
MOM: *I have to be honest and say that I don't like messy jobs, either, like cleaning the bathroom. I can appreciate how Rob feels.*
RALPH: *Me, too.*
DAD: *You're all not in favor of doing unpleasant jobs.*
MOM: *No, but unfortunately they have to be done.*
DAD: *I'm not a lover of unpleasant jobs myself. So we have four people who don't like to do unpleasant jobs, and we don't have a maid around to take out the trash and clean up after the dog. Who has some suggestions about what we might do?*
RALPH: *We could take turns doing them.*
DAD: *Before we decide, maybe we should ask if there are any other unpleasant jobs we really don't like to do.*
ROB: *The toilet, cleaning the bathrooms, like Mom says.*
DAD: *Are there any others?*
RALPH: *There are trash cans, toilets, and the dog. I can't think of any others.*
DAD: *For me dirty dishes are an unpleasant job. So that makes trash, toilets, the dog, and dishes.*
ROB: *Cleaning my room, especially under the bed.*
MOM: *That's true, but who does the room belong to?*

ROB: Me.

DAD: That's right, and Ralph's room belongs to him, and our room belongs to us, so we are responsible for our own rooms. But these other jobs belong to all of us. Ralph, you said we could take turns. How does everybody feel about this? (Family agrees.)

DAD: Has anybody got any suggestions about deciding how we could take turns?

ROB: We could take turns on different days.

DAD: Okay, why don't we brainstorm? Do you all know what brainstorming is?

ROB: Everybody thinks up ideas.

MOM: Right—say everything you can think of, no matter how crazy it sounds.

DAD: Let's just see if we can think of everything we can without stopping to say, "I like that," or, "I don't like that." After we think up some ideas, we can talk about them. What other ideas do we have?

ROB: One person could do one part of the job and another person the other part.

RALPH: We could each take some jobs for a week and then trade.

DAD: I have a suggestion called the job jar. You write each job on a slip of paper and put all of them into a jar. Everyone draws out one at a time until the jar is empty. Each person would do the job he drew for that week, and then, at next week's meeting, we would draw again. (All slips are returned to the jar.) Are there any more suggestions? (Family indicates none.)

DAD: Why don't we go back over all the suggestions we have made so far and decide what we're going to do?

MOM: The first one was trade jobs by days.

RALPH: I don't like that one.

MOM: The next one was splitting the jobs up into parts.

ROB: I like that one.

RALPH: So do I, because that way no one gets stuck with the whole awful job.

DAD: I don't care one way or the other, but it seems to me complicated. It would involve a lot of record keeping.

MOM: I don't feel this is a problem. For instance, one person empties the wastebaskets, the second takes the garbage cans out to the curb, and the third person brings them in. What's complicated about that?

ROB: A week is more complicated. It's really, really unpleasant doing these jobs for a whole week.

DAD: You mean you would prefer to have only part of the job so that you wouldn't be stuck with it for a whole week? How about the rest of the family?

ROB: I kind of like the idea of splitting it up. I don't care for the idea of the whole week on one job.

RALPH: Me, too.

DAD: Well, my only feeling about the whole week was that it was simpler, but if all of you are opposed, I'm willing to forget it. One thing that appeals to me is the job jar, but we could still use it if we put on the slips "Dog papers Thursday morning" or "Trash cans inside Monday night." How do you feel about that?

MOM: Now, let me be sure I understand how this job jar is going to work. Are we going to split the jobs up into parts? That way no one would get stuck with the whole unpleasant job.

ROB: That's what I said—splitting each job up into parts for each day.

DAD: *Well, it seems to me that we have come down to two ideas: the job jar and just choosing parts for the day. Now, what does everyone want to do?*

MOM: *I thought we were talking about using the two together.*

RALPH: *I want the job jar—it sounds more fair.*

ROB: *I like that one, too. It's sort of like a game.*

MOM: *I'm not happy with the job jar because it's easier for me to know that I have certain jobs to do at certain times, but I'm willing to give it a try in order to reach a solution.*

RALPH: *Oh, Dad, what if we pick two jobs for the dog on the same night? Do we have to do them both?*

DAD: *This is the one problem I see with the job jar. I would like you all to consider the element of chance. It is possible that you could draw "Clean up for the dog" four days in one week and the next week you might not draw it at all. You have to consider this as opposed to the idea of signing up and trading equally every week.*

ROB: *I'm willing to take a chance.*

RALPH: *So am I.*

DAD: *It seems to me that we have settled this one, is that right? (Family agrees.)*

DAD: *But we need to decide on what goes on the list, such as outside trash, inside trash, and so forth.*

ROB: *We already decided on that, Dad. Mom has the list.*

DAD: *That's right. Then all we have to do is copy the list and cut up the slips. (Mother prepares the slips for drawing while the discussion continues.)*

DAD: *Any other old business? No? Okay, any new business?*

ROB: *It looks as if we settled quite a few of our*

*problems. How about that family fun you talked
about?*
*DAD: Let's see how everyone else feels. Any other
problems? No? Then how about some entertainment? (Family decides on a movie.)*
DAD: Is there any other new business?
*MOM: Just one thing. This may be old business,
but I would like to say that the boys have really
been helpful this last week in cleaning the base-
ment. I really appreciate it.*
*DAD: I'd like to add that I like the way you boys
did some thinking during our meeting today. Shall
we distribute the allowances and adjourn? (Meeting adjourned.)*

CHORES, AND HOW THE FAMILY MEETING
CAN HELP

Parents often complain that children will not assume responsibility for doing necessary household duties. But the parent will
discover that cooperation is more readily forthcoming from the
child who is given the opportunity to participate in deciding
which task to perform than from the child whose chore is arbitrarily assigned. Family meetings provide the child with an
overall view of what is to be done and give him the responsibility of helping to decide who is to do it. Once the child has been
involved in selecting and agreeing to perform certain duties, it
can be expected that he will fulfill his agreements.

If the child does not perform the agreed-upon duties, logical
consequences should be applied. The concern is discussed at
the next meeting to see if the child wants to do the same job or
make changes. If there is still no cooperation, the parents
should continue using logical consequences. (For further discussion of logical consequences, see chapter 8.)

A General Approach to Breaking Agreements

The following example shows how one father solved the problem of the breaking of agreements.

> At a family meeting Dave and Connie and their two children, Beth, ten, and Bart, nine, had discussed what jobs had to be done around the house. The two children agreed to take care of their rooms, and along with Dave, they agreed to help their mother, who was a full-time university student, with the cleaning each Saturday morning. It was not long before the children began to ignore the agreements.
>
> At a following family meeting Dave discussed the problem with the children. He told them that in his business he used contracts. He explained to them that contracts were like agreements, and in a contract both parties agreed to do certain things. If one of the parties violated the agreement, then the other party was not held to his or her part of the bargain. He applied this to their family situation. If the children did not keep their agreements, then the parents would not be bound by the agreements they had made with the children, such as taking them out on weekends, which was a normal occurrence in their family.

For a while the children kept their agreements. Later, however, they began to neglect their duties. The parents refrained from comment. That Saturday, the children asked their parents if they were going to be taken to the movies as had been agreed. Dave answered, "I'm sorry, but we do not feel like keeping our agreements; we'll see how we feel next weekend."

Dave and Connie reported that they seldom had difficulty in the future.

Dave approached the problem in a logical manner that made sense to the children. When the children again broke their agreements, the parents did not nag or coax but let the consequences take place. They assured the children of another chance. (Consequences are never to be motivated by revenge.)

At What Age Can Children Become Involved in Household Chores?

Many parents wonder at what age children can be expected to do certain chores. This often depends on the attitude of the parents. The parent who feels responsibility to make life comfortable for the child expects very little from the child and usually gets what is expected. On the other hand, the parent who is overzealous tends to expect too much from the child. The parent often resorts to force in an attempt to "make" the child responsible.

The child begins by taking care of his personal belongings. As he begins to mature, he will be able to assume other responsibilities. Parents can help by asking the child to perform certain duties. Many times a three- or four-year-old will enjoy setting the table or help make his own bed and straighten up his room. It is important to capitalize on any indication of a desire to cooperate with chores. A parent's high standards could result in a child who is never "old enough" to cooperate. High standards can tend to create children who display inadequacy and are excused from chores.

ALLOWANCES

Essentially, the reason for giving an allowance is to develop in the child an understanding of the value of money and budgeting. As soon as the child has financial needs for contributions, recreation, or treats, an allowance can be started. The child may be given enough money to cover actual needs plus a small amount for savings. The allowance may then be modified to fit new needs. By the time a child is in second or third grade she may be given enough money each week to cover the cost of lunch, if it is purchased, savings, consumable school supplies, such as paper, pencils, and so on, and spending money.

The purpose and use of the allowance can be discussed at a family meeting. Amounts of spending money can be negotiated. Allowances can be distributed at the conclusion of the family meeting.

At times children may become excessive spenders. If parents allow them to experience the consequences of free spending, much can be learned.

At a family meeting Kurt and Jean discussed an allowance with Dick, their eight-year-old son. The parents had been giving him a small amount of spending money for about a year and had now decided to give him the responsibility for his lunches, school supplies, and savings as well. Kurt and Dick figured the amount necessary for lunch each week and for spending money and then added an extra dollar for savings and school supplies. After a short time Dick began to take his lunch from home and use the allotted lunch money for entertainment. In the next family meeting Father approached Dick.

> FATHER: *I notice you have started to take your lunch instead of buying it. If this is the case, then you won't need weekly lunch money.*
> DICK: *Yes, but sometimes I still like to buy it.*
> FATHER: *Okay. What do you think would be a fair way to work this out?*
> DICK: *Maybe I could buy it about three times a week, and if I don't use the money, I'll return it.*
> FATHER: *Fine. I like that idea.*

Some parents make allowances a battleground by insisting that the child use the allowance for specific purposes, such as savings. This insistence often defeats what they are trying to accomplish. The child who does not save will learn the value of saving when he experiences the consequences of indiscriminate spending.

An allowance can become a battleground if it is used as a reward or punishment for chores accomplished or neglected. It is our feeling that the allowance should have no specific connection with duties the child is expected to perform. Children have a right to share in family responsibilities. But these are separate and distinct. Parents do not get paid for the jobs they do around the house. Children who are paid for what they should be expected to do as contributing members of the family often develop distorted values concerning money and responsibilities. When allowances are used as punishment, the same distortion usually occurs. In other words, withdrawing money for not doing chores is the same as paying for doing expected jobs.

SUMMARY

The family meeting has great potential for improving human relationships. While it requires time, effort, commitment, involvement, and follow-through, it also improves relationships more effectively than any other single procedure. The family meeting teaches all members of the family to live with mutual respect while listening to each other and cooperating. It has been our experience that parents that do not have time for meetings do not have time to teach their children and are missing a valuable opportunity to create a cooperative family. The frequency of family meetings is often a barometer of the family atmosphere. If there are regular meetings, it is less likely that there will be major conflicts. It is vital that the parent take the time to understand and implement the family meeting. Democratic meetings can help suggestions move from the pages of a book into action in your family.

Family meetings can be an effective way to put the parenting concepts you are learning into action. The initial family meeting can be crucial, and it is essential to be respectful, listen to everyone, and reflect the feelings being heard. You may find resistance to beginning meetings. Listen to what is said, be empathic, and discuss whatever it is a particular family member may be resisting. Be alert to meetings that develop a negative tone, seem to last too long, or are being monopolized by one or two members.

8

I WAS RAISED THAT WAY AND TURNED OUT ALL RIGHT: DISCIPLINE THAT WORKS NOW!

THERE IS GENERAL agreement that becoming mature requires a sense of responsibility. Few parents consciously focus on developing responsibility. Many believe you must "teach" responsibility. Punishment, rewards, and bribes become the tools of the "teaching" process. These methods are generally unsuccessful. You cannot "teach" responsibility. You can provide opportunities for the child to become responsible and then encourage positive efforts and redirect ineffective responses.

DEVELOPING RESPONSIBILITY IN CHILDREN

Basic rules for helping children assume responsibility are:

1. Avoid performing tasks a child can do.
This rule is often violated by parents who have high standards and see the child as incapable of meeting them. When a child is first learning to assume responsibility, she may not conform to adult standards. Children often become discouraged and refuse to accept responsibility if parents reject their efforts.

Allow the child to help at every opportunity. Assist her in taking responsibility for dressing herself, making her bed, taking care of her personal belongings, or helping set and clear the table.

2.   Allow time for training.

Many attempts to develop responsibility fail because of poor timing. The worst time to train a child is when there are definite time limits involved, that is, in the middle of a power struggle or right before leaving for a meeting. A relaxed time, perhaps early in the evening or on the weekend, is the best time to help the child learn. The parent is under no pressure and can be patient and encouraging. For example, attempting to train a young child to tie shoes in the morning when you're rushed invites failure. If pressure of time wears on your patience, you're apt to be critical and try to push the child, or you may eventually give in and do it to "save time." The child is likely to become discouraged and refuse to cooperate.

3.   Ask—don't demand.

Making demands on children usually decreases their desire to help out. On the other hand, requesting cooperation by emphasizing the parents' need for assistance and believing the child is able to do it are appealing to many children. The child feels grown up as she discovers she is of real help to her parents. "Mary, this job is difficult, and I sure need your help. Will you help me, please?" If the child refuses, this may be a clue that the relationship is not effective. Therefore, it is best to accept the child's denial and continue to work on improving the relationship. At those times when the child does help, show appreciation. "Thanks, Mary, you made my job much easier."

4.   Use natural and logical consequences.

When a child refuses to perform those tasks that are his or her sole responsibility, the parent needs to stop talking, withdraw from conflict, and let the child experience the consequences of being irresponsible. No one would learn to become responsible if others continually took the responsibility for them. As long as parents perform the duties, the child will not become responsible. In chapter 9 you will discover many natural and logical procedures designed to help children learn to assume responsibility.

As children learn to accept responsibility they begin to enjoy it. They gain confidence and feel worthwhile. Occasional periods of discouragement can be counteracted by reminding them of success in previously performed tasks.

ESTABLISHING RESPECT FOR ORDER

Observing the rules of order holds top priority in any established society, for without order, chaos, violence, and eventual self-destruction may occur. Each parent has an obligation to train the child to respect order. Permissiveness and autocratic methods produce children who have difficulty accepting order and little respect for authority and who are concerned only with their own rights. These children must experience the inconvenience of disorder before they can recognize how authority and the restrictions it imposes are necessary.

When a parent continually tries to force the child to wear a coat in cold weather, the child resists, resenting the parent's authority. If he wears his coat at all, the child may remove it when he is out of his parent's sight. But when the parent stops arguing and reminding and allows the child to experience the discomfort of going without a coat, the child soon learns the value of cooperating.

To resolve conflicts effectively, we must approach them through democratic procedures. Natural consequences, such as the discomfort of going without a coat in cold weather, provide a method for the parent to allow the child to learn from the natural order of events. The parent does not threaten the child, argue, or concede but rather permits the child to discover the advantages of respect for order. By experiencing consequences, the child develops a sense of self-discipline and internal motivation. Children respect order not because they will be punished but because they have learned that order is necessary for effective functioning.[1]

Allowing the child to experience some consequences would be dangerous or harmful. In such cases the parent must develop logical consequences to fit the situation. Be careful not to confuse consequences with punishment.

Logical consequences are arranged by an adult but must be experienced by the child as logical in nature.

1. Logical consequences express the reality of the social order, not of the person; punishment expresses the power of personal authority.

2. The logical consequence is logically related to the misbehavior; punishment rarely is.

3. Logical consequences imply no element of moral judgment; punishment often does.

4. Logical consequences are concerned only with what will happen now; punishment, with the past.

5. The voice is friendly when consequences are invoked; there is danger in punishment, either open or concealed.[2]

The best consequence can be turned into punishment through misapplication. Anger, threats, warnings, or reminding may destroy the effect. In some instances the parent may not verbalize feelings but communicate a punitive attitude nonverbally; she essentially "shouts with her mouth shut."

> Debbie had a problem with ten-year-old Becky. Each washday she would have to prod Becky to put her dirty clothes in the hamper.
> Debbie heard about logical consequences from her neighbor and decided to try this new approach. She told Becky she would wash each Monday only what was in

the hamper. Throughout the week Debbie would hint, "Don't you think you should pick up your dirty clothes?" or "Remember, I said I will only wash what is in the hamper."

Becky complained that she didn't have any clean school clothes to wear. Her mother said, "Since you didn't put anything in the hamper, I guess you'll have to wear your old clothes." Becky grumbled and finally put on an old outfit.

Another week went by, and Becky still did not put her dirty clothes in the hamper, although her mother reminded her several times. When Monday morning came, her mother lost her patience. Angry and frustrated, she demanded that Becky put her clothes in the hamper. Debbie complained to her neighbor that logical consequences had not worked.

Becky had no need to assume the responsibility of getting her clothes washed. She knew her mother "didn't mean it." Debbie's consequence was ineffective because she did not remain firm in her decision. She coaxed, reminded, and finally gave in to her "old ways." Through her irresponsibility, Becky gained control. If Debbie had stated her intentions concerning washday and refrained from all subsequent comments, and if she had allowed her daughter to experience the consequences of her irresponsible behavior, Debbie probably would have gotten results. When Becky complained about having nothing to wear, Debbie could have placed the total responsibility on Becky's shoulders by saying something like "I'm sure you'll figure out what to do." This conveys her faith in Becky's ability to solve the problem and does not give the issue or the child any unwarranted attention.

Consequences must be applied in a friendly manner, with no strings attached. The parent permits the child to choose and accept the responsibility of his or her choice. If the parent uses the consequences with the intention of forcing the child to give in, is unwilling to accept the child's choice, or attempts to manipulate through the consequence, the child will know this and will respond with resistance.

> "Bill, we will eat at six o'clock. If you want to eat supper, you will have to be home around that time." (Bill has been given the option of coming home on time to eat supper or not, as he chooses.)
> Bill tests his mother by coming home after the dishes have been cleared.
> "Where's dinner, Mom?"
> "I'm sorry, Bill, but you decided not to come home in time for supper. Breakfast is in the morning."

The above example shows the results of using consequences and choice. This is different from the typical situation when misbehavior occurs and the parent decides on a punishment that may not relate to the misbehavior.

With the exception of being sent to bed, the same result occurs—hunger. Since his mother had given him a choice and then upheld her decision without moralizing or becoming angry, Bill has a good chance of learning a lesson. If she had become upset or not given him a choice at all, she would have invited retaliation, and no learning would have taken place.

When applying a consequence, it is very important to stay friendly and not retaliate. Like the mother in the example above, you show the child you're interested in helping him, not in making him "pay for his crime." Although you have no guarantee of how the child perceives our actions, you have a much better chance of success if you make him aware you do not enjoy his suffering. When the parent is angry, the child often feels that the parent is rejecting him as a person. When the parent continues to be friendly, the child senses he is valued, even though the behavior is not.

Most of our disciplining is done by coaxing, reminding, threatening, and punishing rather than by simply allowing children to experience the unpleasantness of their actions. While we may believe we are protecting the child, in truth we are denying him a learning experience. Logical consequences make sense to the child because they are what might happen without our interference.

Mike, ten years old, and his father were building a model airplane together. Mike was eager and started right away to try to put pieces together. Father said, "Mike, I think we can do a much better job if we read the instructions first." Mike verbally agreed but began to glue some pieces in place while his father patiently read the instructions. Father refrained from comment and let Mike attack the problem in his own way.

A half hour later, Mike had completed the model except for one piece. Mike tried to put the piece in its place but found that it would not fit.

"Why won't this fit?" wondered Mike out loud. Father did not reply. Mike looked puzzled and turned to his father: "Dad, why can't I make this fit?"

"I think it's because that part had to go in before the piece marked 'fourteen.'"

"Oh, no." Mike sighed. "Can it be fixed, Dad?"

"I'm afraid not, son; the glue has already dried." Mike appeared sad as he looked at the ruined model.

"You seem pretty sad about this," said Father.

"I am," said Mike.

"I know you were looking forward to hanging this up in your room. I'm sure it's disappointing."

"It sure is," replied Mike.

"What do you think we could do the next time to prevent this from happening?" asked Father.

"I guess we'd better follow the directions."

Here Father did not lecture on the virtue of following directions. He made his suggestion, and Mike chose to ignore it. Father let him discover the value of instructions through experience. He used reflective listening to show Mike that he understood how it felt to ruin a project, and he helped Mike learn to avoid the error in the future without being smug and saying, "I told you so."

For consequences to be effective, it is necessary to follow a procedure that is consistent.

1. Verbal choice: "David, you may settle down and watch TV with us or leave the room. You decide."
2. Implementing the child's decision: Child settles down but acts up again. "I see you have decided to leave. Come back when you are ready to settle down."

    When encountering resistance—as when the child refuses to leave—you might say: "Do you want to leave on your own, or should I help you?" If the child does not go, he has decided to leave with help. Firmly but kindly remove him.
3. Repetition of same or similar behavior at another time: "I see you have decided to leave. You can come back when you're ready." If he doesn't go, assume he has decided to leave with help and remove him. Go to get him in about fifteen minutes. "You may come back now." If he decides not to come, leave him.

At succeeding occurrences of the misbehavior say nothing; just remove him. Go to get him in about one-half hour. Increase the amount of time on each repeat of the misbehavior.

A TYPICAL DAY IN FAMILY LIFE

Difficulties often arise out of the daily routine, presenting particularly annoying and recurrent problems for both parents and children. Rather than becoming increasingly frustrated day after day, the parent can put an end to routine disturbances by employing consequences.

Rush Hour

Ruth, a mother who has chosen to not work outside the home, has two boys, Tom, eight, and Steve, six. Every morning was bedlam. Tom would have to be called several times before he would finally get up. Steve would get up on the first call, but then be would constantly cry for his mother's help in picking out his clothes and in getting dressed. Both boys argued during breakfast. They refused to eat whatever their mother had prepared and forced her to provide something different. Many times, because of all the fuss, the boys missed the bus, and their mother had to drive them to school.

Ruth has two very powerful boys who treat her with disrespect. She believes she is responsible for getting her sons off to school. She fails to see how she is depriving them of the necessary experience of learning to be on time.

Ruth has to begin to place the responsibility for "rush hour" where it belongs. First, she provides the boys with alarm clocks and teaches them how to set them. She lets her sons know they are capable of getting up, dressed, fed, and off to school.

Breakfast will be placed on the table. Ruth will call the boys once and give them the choice of eating what is available or not eating, as they prefer. If they refuse to eat, they will experience the natural consequence of being hungry.

If the boys miss the bus, they will have to walk to school and experience the logical consequence of being late. It may be helpful for Ruth to call the teacher and inform her of what she is trying to do, asking for her cooperation in seeing that the boys make up time and work missed.

Ruth must remain firm in her decisions and refrain from reminding, coaxing, nagging, or "shouting with her mouth shut." She must be willing to allow her sons to experience the consequences of being late. After two or three days the boys will probably learn the value of being on time.

Walking to school is appropriate if you live in a safe neighborhood, but what if you don't? Here's one way a stay-at-home dad solved this problem.

> Stuart, six years old, always dawdled in the morning, forcing his dad to get him up, dress him, and rush him out the door just in time for the school bus. Dad decided it was time Stuart learned to be responsible for getting himself off to school. He bought Stuart an alarm clock, taught him to use it, and informed him it was his responsibility to catch the bus in time for school.
>
> The next morning, Stuart overslept and missed the bus. He began to cry, wondering what to do. Dad said, "I guess you will have to stay home, and the only reason for staying home from school is sickness. So I guess you're sick." Stuart complained he was not sick, but his dad stuck to his decision and put Stuart to bed. Still assuming he was sick, he didn't allow him to play with his friends when they came home from school. He must have his rest.
>
> The next morning, Stuart was up and out the door in time for the bus.

The consequence could have backfired easily if Dad had not maintained his resolve. If he had argued with Stuart about his being "sick" or lectured about being on time, the experience might not have been effective.

If you work outside the home, a different approach is needed. Our friend and colleague, Tucson family counselor Oscar C. Christensen, advises parents to tell the child that if she's not dressed in time for them to leave for work, they'll place her clothes in a paper (or plastic) bag and drop the child off at school on the way to work. The child can choose to dress in the car or wear her nightclothes to school. If she doesn't set her alarm or ignores it and is still in bed when it's time to leave, the parents will have to get her up and moving.

Be sure to call the teacher before you do this, explain your reasons for taking this action, and request the teacher's cooperation. You're trying to teach your child responsibility; let the teacher know this is an area of frequent conflict that you want to eliminate. Most teachers will appreciate what you're trying to do. If not, you can talk with the principal.

This procedure works. Children don't want to look bad in front of their peers. Most dress in the car. It usually takes only a day or two for them to get the message. You need to be sure you don't spoil the consequence by too much talk or sending annoying or angry signals. (Some parents have difficulty refraining from laughing, but don't, as this will backfire.)

With older children and teens, you can still buy them the alarm clock, but the bag procedure would be inappropriate. You'll need the cooperation of the school. School personnel will need to arrange consequences at school for youngsters who are late or miss school, such as having them stay after school to make up missed work.

Dinnertime

Dinnertime can be quite hectic in many families. Some children have to be called several times, others refuse to eat certain foods, brothers and sisters misbehave at the table.

One of the ways parents can learn more effective ways to relate to their children is through participating in parent study groups. A parent study group meets on a regular basis with a trained leader to discuss solutions to child-raising problems. (See Appendix C for information on parent study groups.)

At a weekly meeting of a parent study group, problems that occur at mealtime were discussed.

> NANCY: *My two children are always busy playing when dinner is ready. Every night I have to drag them to the table. Both my husband and I are exasperated by the time we sit down to eat.*
> COUNSELOR: *What does the group think is happening in this situation?*
> WALT: *It seems to me the children are in a power*

contest with you and your husband. You want to eat at a certain time, and the children want to eat when they feel like it.

C: I agree. Does anyone have a suggestion as to what might be done?

FRAN: I had the same problem with my seven-year-old. I told him I would call him to the table once. He could come or not come as he chose. If he came to the table while we were still eating, he would be welcome to eat with us. If not, he could join us for breakfast in the morning. He missed dinner twice, and after that he came on time.

DENNIS: We tried that, too, but it didn't work for us because our son would raid the refrigerator, and I ended up fighting with him about snacks.

C: Has anyone else had that problem?

JODI: I had it. My neighbor, who attended the group last term, suggested I tell the children snacks are for those who eat their supper. But my daughter would sneak snacks from the refrigerator. I finally had to buy a lock and a coated chain to put around the refrigerator.

DENNIS: Isn't locking up things drastic? Shouldn't the children learn to stay out of cabinets without the use of locks?

C: I agree it would be better if the children respected your decision. But the problem is that some of them do not. This is generally due to an ineffective relationship. In a good relationship we hear and respect each other. In order to build a good relationship, we have to learn to avoid power struggles. Therefore, at this point it is much better to lock up snacks than to fight about them.

FRAN: How would you approach this with the children?

ELLI: I approached my daughter in the morning before she left for school because this is one of the *calmer times in our house. I said, "It appears you are not yet ready to accept the responsibility for leaving snacks alone. Therefore, I will have to lock the refrigerator. Tomorrow I will take the lock and chain off and see how it goes.*

C.: I think it's important to emphasize the importance of timing. Elli approached her daughter at a time when she was feeling friendly toward her. Approaching a child at or near the time of conflict often heightens the conflict and turns a consequence into a punishment. Except for occasions when the child is causing a disturbance or in a situation that requires immediate attention, it is best to choose a more relaxed time to discuss the problem.

RACHEL: Should children who refuse to eat certain foods be required to eat at least a small portion?

C: Why do you think children refuse to eat certain foods?

JODI: Probably because they don't like them. All of us have our likes and dislikes.

C: That's true, but how many of us have grown to like certain foods we didn't like in childhood?

DENNIS: I think I see what you mean. In other words, children sometimes use food as a weapon—to get parents involved in a power contest.

C: That's my feeling. What do you think can be done about this?

DICK: Perhaps the family could discuss at their family meeting certain foods that the members like and dislike and reach some sort of agreement.

FRAN: What do you mean?

SANDY: For instance, if the children didn't like green beans and the parents did, they could agree on how many nights to serve green beans. They could also decide how many nights to fix what the children like.

FRAN: That sounds like a good idea, but what if

the children won't eat the green beans on the night
they are served?
ELLI: Then the children can eat the other foods, as
long as they don't deprive other members of their
portions.
DONNA: What about children who eat very little
of anything at the table?
JODI: That's their right. They can eat again at
breakfast. Here the "snacks are for those who eat
their meals" would apply.
DONNA: Would the children be allowed their
dessert if they didn't eat enough of the meal?
SANDY: Is dessert part of the meal?
DONNA: Yes, I guess it is.
DICK: Then, in my opinion, it should be treated
just like the other foods served. If we are going to
let the children eat what they wish of what's offered, then they should be allowed the dessert, too.
C: I agree. Too often dessert is used to force children to eat other portions of the meal. I think we
can gain more cooperation from our children if we
don't use dessert as a weapon.

Bedtime

Bedtime presents a problem for many families. The parents
want the children to go to bed so that they may have some time
to themselves, and the children want to stay up, thinking that all
kinds of magical things go on after they are in bed.

Jenny, nine, Greg, seven, and Neil, five, kept the house
in an uproar at bedtime by getting up for drinks, making
noises, and arguing. Out of desperation, their mother
and father usually gave each child a spanking and then
waited through the additional time the children spent
crying until the house finally became quiet. This process
began at 8:30 P.M. and ended approximately an hour

later. In the morning all three children seemed rested despite the preceding night's battle.

These parents are in a losing battle with their children. First of all, many children do not need as much sleep as we think. If the child can function the next day on less sleep than the parent originally determines, then he has not made the best judgment of the child's requirements. It is generally advisable to establish separate and individual bedtimes related to the age of each child. The bedtimes can be negotiated with the children. With separate bedtimes, the negative interactions among the children will be eliminated, and the negotiations will provide an opportunity for the parent to communicate with each child individually and in a positive fashion.

If you can't elicit cooperation by making agreements, then you may employ consequences. By being allowed to stay up as late as he pleases, the child will undoubtedly experience the natural consequences of not having enough sleep until he learns to go to bed at a reasonable hour.

CONSEQUENCES FOR COMMON CONCERNS

The principles of logical consequences are highly effective in dealing with a variety of behaviors and issues that parents are likely to encounter as their children grow up.

Forgetfulness

Many parents find forgetfulness quite disturbing. They wonder why some children seem unable to remember anything. As with all behavior and misbehavior, forgetfulness is best understood by looking at how it is used and at its results.

Susie seems to forget everything. Each morning, she dashes out to the bus only to have her dad call to remind her to take her schoolbooks and other materials.

Looking at the consequences of Susie's forgetting, the purpose becomes clear. Susie does not have to remember; her father does it for her. Susie has discovered an effective way of gaining her father's attention and service. If Susie's father would tell her she is old enough to be responsible for remembering what to take to school, Susie would have to deal with the teacher, who would probably lend her books and materials only the first few times.

Eleven-year-old Barry's parents were divorced. Barry lived with his father. At a family meeting, Barry agreed to take out the trash each Tuesday and Thursday, but he always forgot. Father would remind him before he left the house, but a few minutes later he would forget to do it. Father then began to watch to make sure he did not forget.

It appears that Barry does not want to keep the agreement. His forgetting is an attempt to try to avoid his job. If his father is to cure Barry's forgetfulness, he must relinquish the responsibility of making sure Barry remembers. And since it is apparent that Barry does not wish to keep this agreement, Dad will discuss the problem with him in an effort to reach an alternative. Dad will hear Barry's feelings, send I-messages, and work out a new agreement that is acceptable to both.

> DAD: *Barry, it seems to me you really don't like the agreement we made about the trash.*
> BARRY: *I don't.*
> DAD: *I can understand how you feel. I know it's an unpleasant job.*
> BARRY: *Those cans are heavy and dirty and smelly. I just hate that job!*
> DAD: *You're really angry about this.* [Hearing feelings]
> BARRY: *Yeah!*
> DAD: *I can appreciate how you feel, but I have a*

problem, too. I don't feel it's fair for me to have to do all the jobs in our house. How can we work this out? Is there some way both of us can be satisfied? [Exploring alternatives]
BARRY: Maybe if we took turns taking out the trash, it wouldn't be so bad.
DAD: Okay, but I still feel this would be putting an extra job on me, considering all the other things I have to do. [I-message]
BARRY: I could help with the dishes once in a while.
DAD: That sounds good to me. I feel good when we listen to each other, because it improves our relationship. [I-message]

Here Dad has made an attempt to deal with the problem in a constructive way. He approached Barry in a friendly manner and gave him a chance to express his feelings concerning the problem. He used reflective listening to show Barry he understands how Barry feels. Dad expressed his own feelings through I-messages. Together they worked out a mutually agreeable solution. Dad has a good chance of winning cooperation. However, if Barry still persists in not keeping his agreements, Dad may have to utilize consequences or renegotiate to resolve the conflict.

When children habitually forget, look at the purpose. Then you can select appropriate responses. In situations where the forgetting does not directly affect you, withdraw and let the natural consequences take place. In situations where the child's forgetting poses a problem for you, hear the child's feelings, express your own feelings, reach agreement, and then, if necessary, utilize consequences.

Kitchen Chores

Pat, ten, had agreed at a family meeting to set the table each evening. For the next few days the agreement was kept. Toward the end of the week, however, Pat began to "forget" her commitment. Mother had to remind and coax her.

It appears that Pat is not yet willing to keep her agreement. Mother is kept busy reminding and coaxing. The responsibility for the chore at this point belongs to Mother.

If Mother wishes to help Pat assume responsibility, she will need to stop talking and act. She will have to utilize logical consequences to help Pat see the effects of irresponsibility.

Instead of reminding and coaxing, Mother can state her intentions. When she notices that the table has not been set, she can leave the kitchen and occupy herself with other pursuits. When Pat asks about dinner, she could say, "I can't serve dinner because the table isn't set." While it may seem unfair for the rest of the family to wait for their dinner, if Mother begins reminding and coaxing, Pat will not learn to assume responsibility.

A responsible person anticipates and does what needs to be done. If the family is to be a unit, each member must make a contribution for the good of all.

The consequences Mother used in the above table-setting example can also be used when a child breaks an agreement to empty the kitchen wastebasket. If the trash begins to pile up, Mother can state her intentions: "I'm sorry, but I don't like to work in a kitchen where there's a lot of garbage."

When you state an intention, the statement must always be backed up with action in order to be effective. You need only state your intentions once. Repeated statements lose their effect. Action is effective; talk usually is *not*.

Children's Rooms

One of the most difficult problems to solve is the care of children's bedrooms. Parents are constantly reminding children to keep their rooms neat. When parents have an ineffective relationship with their child, the child often becomes uncooperative in areas that are most important to the parents. Neatness often becomes one such issue with parents who find it very difficult to tolerate messy rooms.

As with hairstyles and taste in clothing, many children feel they have a right to keep their rooms as they wish. Parents stand a better chance of influencing their child toward orderliness if they respect the child's room as a personal responsibility. Creating battlegrounds over rooms seldom teaches children to be neat. The children may continue to keep their rooms messy to show parents that they can't be forced to be neat. It's best to withdraw from such a power contest.

Parents recognize the child's right to maintain his own room the way he wishes. The bedroom door can be closed if the mess bothers the parents. Without the parents' distress over the room's condition, the child can gain no payoff for his misbehavior and often becomes tired of the mess, too. This usually takes quite a long time, however.

Parents have rights also. You have the right not to enter the child's room to change the sheets if you don't like the mess. You can tell the child you're not willing to enter a room that is messy. You can leave the clean sheets outside the room for the child to take care of. If he does not change the sheets after a reasonable time, you can assume he does not want them and put away the clean sheets.

In cases where you've agreed at a family meeting to clean the child's room if it is "in order," you can refuse to clean the room if the child has not straightened it up.

Television

Television is often blamed for many difficulties. It interferes with the children's chores, homework, and bedtime, they contend. Interestingly enough, however, when the parents turn off the television set, they often still experience much difficulty in getting the jobs done. Many children use television to evade, put off, or "forget" what they are supposed to do. By doing so they are sending the parents a message: "I don't intend to do what you want me to if I can help it." Therefore, when parents find that television is interfering with their children's responsibilities, it is time to examine the relationship.

Some parents create battlegrounds over television by arbitrarily restricting its use. This approach often causes resentment and retaliation on the part of the children. Also, parents are often inconsiderate of children's wishes in regard to favorite programs. Many parents resent their child's interference when they are watching a favorite movie. Yet these same parents think nothing of demanding that a certain chore or task be done immediately, whether or not the child is watching a program.

If parents wish to gain the children's cooperation regarding the use of television, as in any other area of conflict, they must take the children's interests and preferences into consideration. This can be an opportunity to share feelings and values and reach mutually agreed-on decisions.

Some children occupy most of their time watching television. These children may be using television to escape reality. They prefer and feel more comfortable in the fantasy world of television. In this case, discuss with the child the amount of time spent watching television and come to an agreement about how much time each day can be spent this way. Then the child may select the programs he wishes to watch during his "TV time."

An exception to permitting children to watch programs they want during their TV time involves violent programs. Many parents are concerned about violence on TV. This needs to be discussed with the children. Programs that are unacceptable to you should not be part of the children's choice of what to watch during their TV time. Be aware, though, of any violent content in the programs you choose to watch. Children learn from your model.

Another approach to violent programming is to watch such programs with the children and discuss the reasons the producers decide to air such programs as well as why the children like to watch them. Some questions to discuss are: Do the producers believe violence is the only way to make a program exciting? Do they think people want violence and that it "sells"? Do the children want to watch the programs because they're exciting? What are some other ways to make life exciting? How does violence on TV compare to violence in real life? How are they similar, and how are they different? What's fantasy, and what's reality?

At times, parents will restrict television viewing as a punishment in order to force the children to do what is expected of them. Children who bring home poor report cards or refuse to do their chores are often denied the privilege of watching television. This approach is usually ineffective, as is any retaliatory act, and often invites further misbehavior.

The same approaches for TV watching can be used with the family computer. While computers can help children learn, they can also be misused. Some children avoid involvement with others by developing a relationship with the computer. Other children play violent computer games. If you're concerned about these issues, discuss them with the child and set guidelines on use of the computer.

Care of Personal Belongings

"Scott and Janet, you come here this minute!" shouted Mother. "Now, pick up these toys. Why do I always have to tell you to pick up after yourselves?"

This scene is not uncommon. Parents often complain that children strew their possessions about the house, leaving them with the unpleasant choice of having to keep after the children to pick things up or do the chore themselves. What these parents don't realize is that they can approach the problem in a variety of effective ways. Here's a way one parent solved the problem.

Becky has three children—Mike, fourteen, Joan, ten, and Sharon, five. The children would often neglect to put their belongings away.

At the supper table Becky said to her children,

"When I find your things scattered around the house, I feel exhausted. From now on I'll put the things I find into a box in the garage. If you are missing anything, you can look in the box."

Becky approached the problem in a friendly spirit. She did not lecture and preach to the children about how they should pick up things. She used an I-message to convey to them how she feels about the situation and stated her intentions. It was up to the children to decide if they wished to put their belongings away or search through the box. In most cases children become tired of rummaging through a box every time they want something they have carelessly left lying around, and they begin to pick up after themselves.

Another way of approaching the problem is to put the objects away. When the children ask for something, they are told that it appears they have not yet learned to put things away and so they may not have the object, but they may try again the next day. After the allotted time the child is given back the article. If he continues to leave things out of place, then his belongings will be removed for two days, and so on.

Clothing and Grooming

Many parents today are greatly concerned about the clothing and hairstyles of their children, especially teenagers. Each generation of preteen and teenage children in the past several decades has had its own particular style of appearance, dictated by peer acceptance rather than adult approval. Parents tend to create battlegrounds over fads, forgetting that the clothes they wore as youngsters once annoyed their own parents.

Joy, thirteen, and her dad often argued intensely over what Joy was to wear to school. Dad complained that he did not approve of his daughter's choice of clothing, while Joy bitterly responded that all her friends dressed in this particular fashion and that she would have no friends if she wasn't allowed to dress accordingly. Dad said he was not concerned with what Joy's friends wore. "No daughter of mine is going to look like a tramp!" Dad usually succeeded in making Joy wear what he considered proper. But each argument ended in intense negative feelings between Dad and daughter.

Dad may win the battle over what Joy wears, but he may also damage his relationship with his daughter. Creating battlegrounds over minor issues often hampers parental influence in major situations. Why was Dad so concerned about how Joy dressed for school? It appears he felt that Joy's appearance was a reflection on him. Thus, his concern for his own prestige impairs his relationship with his daughter. In actuality, Joy's dress can be regarded as an expression of herself and her own tastes; in no way does it reflect upon her dad.

Cleanliness

Brushing teeth, washing hands, and taking baths create problems for many families. Logical consequences need to be arranged in order to impress upon the children the necessity of keeping clean.

> Frank, six years old, would not brush his teeth in the morning before school. Mother discussed the problem with a friend, who reported she had solved the same problem by telling her children that since sweets cause tooth decay, she would have to discontinue providing sweets if they were not willing to brush their teeth.
> Frank's mother decided to give this a try. One evening before bedtime, Mother told Frank about sweets, tooth decay, and brushing. The next morning, however, Frank did not brush his teeth. That afternoon, after school, Frank asked for a snack. Mother told him that he could have a piece of celery or a carrot. "Why can't I have some cookies?" asked Frank.

"I'm sorry, but you didn't brush your teeth this morning" was his mother's reply.

"Well, can I have an apple?" Frank asked.

Mom replied, "I'm sorry, but apples have sugar in them, too."

Frank grudgingly accepted a carrot.

For the next few days Frank remembered to brush his teeth. Then he began to "forget" again. When he came home from school, he would ask for his treat. Mother would offer him a carrot. "Why can't I have some cookies? I brushed my teeth this morning." Mother knew that he had not. She did not answer, handed Frank a carrot, and left the room.

Getting children to take baths is another trouble spot in many homes. Parents can influence their children without conflict by creating logical consequences that will impress the children with the necessity of taking baths. If the family is going out for an evening, they can refuse to take the children unless they are clean. (You need to plan ahead for a sitter if you're going to use this approach.) But family outings do not usually occur as often as baths are needed. One father solved the bath problem like this:

> Jan, seven years old, had a distaste for bathing and would go for several days without a bath. One night while the family was watching television, Father said, "I'm sorry, Jan, but you have an odor. If you wish to stay here with us, you'll have to bathe." Jan grudgingly left the family room, bathed, and rejoined the family.

This approach is risky, for the child may view it as insulting. However, Jan's father did offer her a choice. He did not order her to bathe; he told her that if she wished to remain with them, she would have to bathe.

An alternate approach to the bathing problem is to prohibit putting clean clothes on a dirty body.

Kevin, nine years old, would seldom bathe without constant nagging from Mother. One morning when Kevin was getting ready for school, Mother said, "I'm sorry, Kevin, but you can't put clean clothes on a dirty body. You'll have to wear dirty clothes." Kevin decided to bathe.

If Kevin had decided to wear the dirty clothes, Mother could have respected his right to choose the alternative. If he continued to choose not to bathe and wear dirty clothes, his peers would most likely begin to let him know how they felt about his appearance and odor. He would probably then have decided to bathe.

Carelessness

Jenny, nine years old, was very careless. One wintry day she lost her gloves at school. Her mother was angry and lectured Jenny on the value of the gloves and the necessity to make sure they were firmly tucked into her coat pocket. Then she called the school and inquired if anyone had found the gloves. Finally, since Mother did not want Jenny to have cold hands, she bought her daughter another pair of gloves.

Jenny has her mother in her control. As long as she is willing to put up with Mother's scolding, she does not have to assume the responsibility of looking after her possessions. For no matter what happens, even an angry mother will take care of the problem.

Mother can learn to place the responsibility for Jenny's belongings on Jenny's shoulders. Next time she might handle the situation this way:

> MOTHER: *I'm sorry you lost your gloves, Jenny.*
> JENNY: *What am I going to do?*

*MOTHER: I don't know, but I'm sure you will
figure something out.
JENNY: Will you buy me another pair?
MOTHER: I'm sorry, but I don't feel I should
spend more money on gloves. If you want to spend
your allowance money, I'll be glad to take you to
the store with me the next time I go.*

In this example, Mother helps Jenny realize she must be responsible for her own possessions. She refuses to become angry and assume ownership of the problem while at the same time she offers Jenny a choice of buying new gloves with her own money or going without. Jenny must make the decision. The consequences of her carelessness will undoubtedly influence her behavior more than Mother's anger and instant solutions of the past.

When children lose or break things, you can use consequences appropriate to the situation. For example, if the child loses or breaks one of his own possessions, he may replace it with his own money or go without; it is his problem. It is not your problem if the child breaks or loses something that belongs to a sibling. It is a problem to be resolved between the children. If the broken or lost object belongs to you, the child would be required to make restitution.

RELATIONSHIPS WITH FRIENDS, NEIGHBORS, AND RELATIVES

When parents have a problematic relationship with their children, the children often display uncooperative behavior in situations where the parents are most vulnerable, such as in the presence of friends, neighbors, or relatives.

Some parents who apply our methods with their children when they are at home may tend to discard them and return to ineffective means when others are present. This usually happens because the parent is concerned with impressing, being accepted, being in control, and not deviating from the expectations of friends or relatives. When questioned as to why they do this, replies such as "Jim's mother would not understand the new ways" or "What would my neighbor think?" are often heard. We ask such parents, "What do you consider more important, impressing others or your relationship with your children?"

> Bob, six years old, had a fight with a neighborhood boy in the churchyard after services. He ran to his mother crying. Realizing the purpose of his act, his mother decided to ignore his bid for attention and pity. "I know that hurts, Bob," she said, and made no further comment. Another mother standing near the scene inquired why Bob's mother did not attend to the matter, as the boy seemed hurt. Before Mother could reply, Bob's father comforted Bob's hurt feelings by drawing him close and telling him everything would be all right. He was quite upset with his wife's actions.
>
> Later, Dad admitted he probably would not have been as concerned if others had not been on the scene.

The real reason for Dad's concern was his imagined loss of status in the eyes of bystanders. Bob's mother, on the other hand, showed Bob that she understood how he felt, but she refused to become involved. She realized overplaying such a situation might pave the way for similar misbehavior in the future. Had Dad not interfered, Bob would have learned that fighting does not win sympathy and special attention.

Danger

In danger or emergency situations it is obvious that one cannot allow the child to experience the natural consequences of behavior. Logical consequences, however, can still be used.

Eight-month-old Grant was crawling on the living-room floor. In his curiosity he began to pull on a lamp cord. Mother jumped up from her chair, grabbed Grant, and gave him a swat, saying, "No, no."

A few minutes later, Grant again approached the lamp cord. Again Mother grabbed him, spanked, and yelled. She then put Grant in his playpen.

Little Grant certainly did not enjoy being spanked, but it appears that he enjoyed the attention he received from Mother by his actions! Why didn't Mother simply put Grant in his playpen the first time he touched the lamp cord? Certainly Mother did not want Grant to be hurt, but from her reaction it seems she also had another motive, teaching Grant to obey her. Again, "Do what I say because I say it" is usually ineffective. If Mother wants to teach Grant to leave the lamp cord alone, she will have to change her approach.

Eight-month-old Grant was crawling on the living-room floor. In his curiosity he began to pull a lamp cord. Mother picked Grant up and placed him in his playpen.

A few minutes later, she took him out of the pen. Grant crawled around and again approached the lamp cord. Mother again placed him in the pen, but this time she left him in for a longer time. When Grant was let out again, he amused himself with a toy.

By her action Mother has shown Grant that if he wishes to have the freedom of the living room, he must stay away from the lamp cord.

Grant responded favorably because he decided he would rather be outside the pen than play with the socket.

It was a nice day, and Tammi, four years old, wanted to play outside. Mother told her that she could go outside as long as she stayed in the yard. She then explained to

Tammi that she did not want her to go into the street because she might get hit by a car.

A few minutes later, she noticed that Tammi had ventured into the street. Mother came from the house and led Tammi by the hand back into the yard. She then asked her daughter, "Would you like to play in the yard or would you like to play in the house?" Tammi said she would rather play in the yard. Mother went back into the house and watched Tammi from the window. Tammi played in the yard for a few minutes and then stepped into the street. Mother went outside and said to Tammi, "I see that you have decided to play in the house. You can go outside later, and then we'll see if you are ready to stay in the yard." Tammi began to cry and said that she did not want to come in. Mother said, "Do you want to come in on your own, or shall I help you?" Tammi made no response. Mother then took her by the hand and led her into the house.

About a half hour later Tammi asked Mother if she could play outside in the yard again. Mother said, "Not right now. We'll try a little later to see if you are ready." About ten minutes later Tammi asked again, and Mother said yes. Mother again watched from the window. Tammi seemed to be content to play in the yard. A while later, however, Mother looked out the window and saw that Tammi was again in the street. Mother went outside, took Tammi by the hand, and led her into the house. When they reached the house, Mother said, "We will try again tomorrow, Tammi."

Here Mother has approached the problem in a matter-of-fact way. She remained calm, gave Tammi a choice, and acted on Tammi's decision. Mother was both firm and kind.

If, after receiving another chance the following day, Tammi still goes into the street, Mother will have to restrict her from the yard for a longer time.

THINGS TO REMEMBER WHEN APPLYING LOGICAL CONSEQUENCES

Logical consequences hold children accountable for their choices. To review, a logical consequence:

- Shows mutual respect.
- Is firm and kind.
- Provides choices.
- Is concerned with what will happen now, not what happened in the past.
- Involves no moral judgment.
- Relates to the logic of the situation.
- Separates the deed from the doer.

MORE CONSEQUENCES FOR TYPICAL CHALLENGES[3]

CHALLENGE	CONSEQUENCE
Spending allowance before next allowance day.	Provide an adequate allowance and let child experience consequences of not budgeting money.
Not doing chores.	Discuss sharing chores at family meeting. General consequences for not doing chores is not going out or engaging in fun activities until chores are done.
Tattling.	Tell child that what she's telling you is really none of your business. From that point on, ignore the tattling. (Children know the difference between tattling and telling you when something dangerous is happening.)
Misbehavior in the car.	Pull over to the side of the road. Tell the children that their behavior is distracting. You'll continue when they settle down.
Whining.	Ignore. Attend to child when he's speaking in a normal voice.
Not feeding pets.	Establish rule. Pets fed before child fed. Consequence: child's meal delayed.
Teen doesn't put gas in family car after she uses it.	Assuming you've discussed "gassing up," teen doesn't use car next time.
Insults.	Acknowledge feelings; state your feelings in I-message. "I understand you're angry, but I won't tolerate being talked to like that." Then ignore further outbursts. Leave room if need be. Discuss feelings later when both have calmed down.

9

REFLECTIVE LISTENING, I-MESSAGES, EXPLORING ALTERNATIVES, CONSEQUENCES . . . HOW DO I DECIDE WHAT TO DO WHEN?

L ISTEN TO THEIR feelings, tell them how you feel, help them decide what to do when they own a problem, negotiate problems you own, give them a choice and let them experience the natural or logical consequences. Good advice, but it's not always easy to decide which approach to use. That's what we'll concentrate on in this chapter—how to decide what to do when. We'll also discuss how to apply the approaches to some tough challenges, like sex, drugs, and violence.

SELECTING APPROACHES

Here's a review of the four approaches we've discussed in *Raising a Responsible Child*.

> Approach 1: Reflective listening—for when the child owns the problem.
> Approach 2: I-messages—for when you own the problem.
> Approach 3: Exploring alternatives—for child-owned problem and for negotiation when you own the problem.

Approach 4: Natural and logical consequences—natural consequences for child-owned problems, logical consequences for child- or parent-owned problems, depending on the particular problem.

The parent's choice of approach will largely depend on the situation. Sometimes all approaches may be necessary; at other times, perhaps only one or two will be needed.

Situations that might involve all the approaches include parent-child conflicts concerning chores, allowance, what time to come home, television, and so on. For example, you and your child may disagree about sharing the chores. You voice the problem at a family meeting. It's discussed, using reflective listening, I-messages, and exploring alternatives. A final agreement is reached but not kept by the child. You use natural or logical consequences for the broken commitments. At the next meeting, renegotiation takes place involving more reflective listening, I-messages, and exploring alternatives. During the discussion a new decision is reached, or the family decides to keep the original agreement. If the child still does not keep his agreements, continue to use consequences.

Many similar situations may be resolved without resorting to the fourth approach: consequences. After renegotiation, the child may keep his agreements. In general, as the relationship improves, you'll find that it becomes less and less necessary to use natural and logical consequences. The child will have more respect for you, and she'll know that you'll employ a consequence if necessary. Thus she may decide to modify her behavior before that step is reached.

Reflective listening and exploring alternatives are used when the child has a problem or when the parent and the child seek mutual agreement. However, if reflective listening and exploring alternatives are overused, they'll provide excess attention and only serve to reinforce the child's purpose. If the child shows no indication of solving the problem through these methods, it may be a clue that the child is using the problem just to gain attention.

> Ten-year-old Jill complained about her teacher. Mom listened, reflecting Jill's feelings. Then they discussed alternatives. But Jill brought the problem home again the next day. Again Mom listened and helped Jill decide what she could do. On the third day, Mom decided that Jill had no sincere desire to solve the problem.
>
> When Jill began to cover the same ground again, Mom said, "Jill, we've discussed this same problem for three days, and it appears that you're not quite ready to approach the situation differently. When you decide you really want to change your approach, I'll be glad to help."

An alternative response could be Mom's declaration of her inability to help while at the same time showing faith in the child: "I guess I can't help you with this, Jill, but I'm sure in time you'll figure it out."

It's best to use I-messages sparingly. Constant reliance on them may trap you into giving negative attention or involve you in a power struggle. Or the child may become tired of hearing your feelings and just stop listening altogether.

When an I-message fails to produce results, you could use consequences or explore alternatives. If you decide to use consequences, be careful not to approach the task with a revengeful attitude: "You don't respect my feelings? Then I'll make you do it." You'll probably encounter immediate resistance and in the long run impede future cooperation. To be effective, consequences must be employed in a spirit of friendliness. Like the I-message, the consequence creates a problem for the child. He has to decide how he wishes to respond—whether he wants to remedy the situation or experience the consequences. You're interested in doing what the situation demands, not in gaining personal power. Your tone of voice and attitude can convey the proper respect for your child.

Lily is moving a cabinet door back and forth with her foot.

DAD: I'm getting concerned that those door hinges will get loose and then the door won't close properly.

Lily stops momentarily but starts again.

DAD: I'm sorry, Lily. You can stop doing that or you can leave the room. You decide.

Here Dad sent an I-message that was ineffective. He then employed a logical consequence, offering the child a choice in a firm but friendly manner. The child will have to make her decision.

In some situations the parent may rely totally on consequences. Getting up in time for school is an example. The parent can provide the child with an alarm clock and give him the responsibility of getting up, dressing, and getting to the breakfast table and to school on time. If he's late, he will have a problem with the teacher; the parent shouldn't be involved. (This procedure is discussed fully in chapter 8.) Some other circumstances when it's best to avoid I-messages and let the consequences take place are fighting between siblings, doing homework, the child's relationship with his other parent, forgetting, and carelessness.

In some instances the parent may decide it's best to ignore the misbehavior. Ignoring is a form of logical consequence, since in order to gain the parent's attention the child will have to alter his behavior. He desires to involve his parent but can't do so as long as he misbehaves. The parent demonstrates his willingness to give the child attention only for useful behavior.

Other practical factors may influence a parent's choice of approach. He may wish to use consequences rather than dialogue because the misbehavior provides consequences that the parent is unwilling to accept. Timing may be a factor. Early in the morning the parent may not have time to respond with I-messages. The parent's physical condition may make discussion too uncomfortable. There may be areas of extreme conflict that need immediate attention. Or perhaps previous experience with dialogue in these situations has proved to be ineffective.

WHAT ABOUT TEENAGERS?

Many of the examples in this book have concentrated on younger children. You may be wondering if the same approaches apply to teens. The answer is yes. What we've been teaching you is just good human-relationship skills applicable to all humans regardless of age.

Nevertheless, parents often dread their children's entrance into the teen years. They believe that their influence is about at an end and that the peer group will become the parent. They fear rebellion, sex, drugs, gangs. These can be realistic fears if the relationship between parent and child has been at odds. But when the relationship has been one of mutual respect, such fears are exaggerated. Earlier we said that the "child is the parent of the adult." We can also say that the "child is the parent of the teen." The relationship you develop with your children when they're young carries over into your relationship with them as teenagers.

True, your relationship will change to a certain extent as teens venture more out in the world on their journey toward adulthood. This is natural. Teens need to develop their own identities and to separate from their parents. But this separation can be one of rejoicing rather than regret: it all depends on how you look at it.

Teens and Rebellion

A rebellious child becomes a rebellious teen. If you've had frequent power contests with your child, they'll most likely continue into his teen and adult years. You may have experienced some victories over your children when they were younger; you were bigger and stronger. But that changes as they get bigger and stronger.

Teen rebellion can be handled in much the same way as power contests with younger children—refuse to fight or give in. This is a time to use exploring alternatives; and in most cases consequences need to be negotiated with teens. (This is also true with older children and preteens.)

Not all consequences need to be negotiated, however.[1] If a problem is minor (such as the teen playing his radio loud—you could just say, "Either turn down the radio or turn it off; you decide") or if a problem is so serious there can be no negotiation. For example, you discover that your teen has been driving drunk; the driving privileges are suspended until such time as you're convinced it won't happen again. (Of course, if you suspect that alcohol is a problem for your teen, get some professional help.)

But there's middle ground for negotiation. Questions such as "What would you do if you were me?" and "What would be a fair consequence in this situation?" can lead to a productive discussion.[2]

As with younger children, the democratic approach works best. You give them increasing independence along with increasing responsibility. You listen, encourage, and expect them to do their share. Listen to their opinions. Seek their advice on things they know well.

Sharon, seventeen, had a part-time job and had saved up for a car. She couldn't afford many of the repairs she had to make, so she learned how to work on the car herself. In a few months' time, Sharon had become a pretty fair mechanic.

Dad's car had a squeak that was driving him nuts. His knowledge about the mechanics of a car was pretty limited. He asked Sharon to take a look at it.

"Loose fan belt, Dad. Simple job. You get one and I'll change it for you."

"No kidding, that simple, huh? Well, you could've

fooled me; I thought it was something serious. Thanks, Sharon. I really appreciate your help."
Sharon beamed.

Dad was smart. He utilized Sharon's talent. He helped her feel important and needed.

There are many other issues with teens too numerous to cover in a general book about parenting. If you have a teenager and want more information, we suggest the following books: *Parenting Teenagers* (from the STEP/teen parent education program) by Don Dinkmeyer and Gary D. McKay (Circle Pines, Minn.: American Guidance Service, 1990; distributed to bookstores by Random House) and *I'm on Your Side: Resolving Conflict with Your Teenage Son or Daughter* by Jane Nelsen and Lynn Lott (Rocklin, Calif.: Prima, 1990).

SELECTING APPROACHES TO SPECIFIC CHALLENGES

The remainder of this chapter will focus on deciding what approaches can be used with various parenting challenges.

Sibling Arguments and Fights

Arguing and fighting among siblings is so common that it is often accepted as normal. But this is certainly not the case. Like all misbehavior, fighting is purposive. Some children fight to gain attention from parents; others, to show parents that they can do what they want, even in defiance of their parents' wishes. And some children pick on a favored child to seek revenge on parents. Our expectations play such an important role in children's fighting that we accept it as normal and expect it; children make a special effort not to let us down. Many of us set examples of human relationships filled with conflict. We argue with our spouse, neighbors, and children, and our children follow our example. In some families conflict is almost a family value.

There are many ways parents try to handle children's squabbles. Maybe you've tried a few of them. When children argue or fight with one another, parents may:

- Lecture: "Come on, you two, can't you learn to get along? Brothers are supposed to love each other."
- Give orders: "Knock it off!"
- Play detective: "All right, who started it?"
- Blame the older child: "Mark, you know better than to hit your little brother! See, you've made him cry."
- Blame the boy (in fights between brothers and sisters): "Tim, you know boys don't hit girls!"
- Punish both children: "All right, you two, no TV until you learn to get along!"
- Try to negotiate: "Okay, let's see if we can work this out between the two of you. Martha, you tell me your side, and then I'll listen to you, Scott."

Most parents find such efforts futile. Lecturing usually goes in one ear and out the other. (You're often telling them what they already know and have decided to ignore.) Giving orders may work for a short while. Playing detective leaves you without a clue, as both "suspects" have their own version of the "truth." Besides, it really doesn't matter who started the conflict. Chances are things happened that you're unaware of, before the actual confrontation occurred. Blaming the older child just because he's older lets a lot of younger kids off the hook. Younger siblings are quite adept at goading their older brothers and sisters because they know you'll protect them. The same is true of blaming the boy. This teaches girls that they can do whatever they want to boys and the parent will step in. Punishing both children only creates resentment and charges of unfairness by both contestants; they'll usually get even with you. Finally, if you play the role of negotiator, you assume ownership of their problem.

Okay, so none of these methods solves the problem. What can you do? Children learn not to argue or fight only when the parent refuses to become involved in the squabbles. Parent involvement in sibling rivalries only increases the conflict. No matter how objective the parent feels he is, from at least one child's point of view, and perhaps from all of them, he is unfair. You can let the natural consequences occur. Arguments don't solve anything and invite hurt feelings on both sides.

This is also true of physical fights. If you think your children won't be seriously hurt by each other, they can learn from the discomfort of physical confrontation.

If you think physical confrontation will result in harm, use logical consequences. "I'm afraid someone is going to get hurt. So you can handle this problem with no hitting or be separated until you're both ready to behave peacefully." Do this matter-of-factly, without threat or blame. If they continue to be physical, act on their choice—to be separated.

In the case of large size or age differences, you can remove the younger or smaller child from the scene. Again, be matter-of-fact about it: "Come on, Danny, let's go find something for you to do." This stops the fight without punishing the older—or younger—child.

Realize that when you remove yourself as a reinforcer of fighting—lecturing, ordering, blaming, etc.—the squabbles may get worse before they diminish in intensity. The children may try to get you back into the fray by tattling. Some may go so far as to feign injury. When this happens, tell the child that the problem is between herself and her sister or brother and you're confident she can handle it. Avoid playing the role of judge and simultaneously instill in the child faith in her own problem-solving abilities.

As you hold weekly family meetings in which problems are discussed and ironed out, your children will learn how to explore alternatives. (See chapter 7 for details on family meetings.) This model can influence their means of settling conflicts between themselves, too.

The location of the argument or fight is often of concern to parents. When children are fighting in their own rooms or in other areas acceptable to the parent, the parent can remove

himself without any comment. The late psychiatrist and teacher
Rudolf Dreikurs told parents to go to the bathroom when children fight. Why? To remove themselves as reinforcers to the
most private place in the house. Parents would often find the
squabble moving to outside the bathroom door—further proof
that fighting is often for the parents' benefit! A radio or small
portable TV helps drown out the noise.

However, if they are fighting in areas that are dangerous or
endangering family property, you can inform them that they can
fight if they wish, but they will have to fight in a spot that you
designate. Often this action alone will stop the fight. By not
denying the children the right to fight and by refusing to become involved and stop the battle, the purpose of the fight can't
be achieved. But as soon as the parent misuses this approach in
an attempt to "make" the children stop fighting, failure is likely.
Attitude is most important.

One last point about children's fights and arguments. Be
sure to reinforce cooperation. When you see them getting
along, comment on it: "I see you two are having fun. Looks like
you're working things out." Avoid praise and judgments like "It's
so nice to see you getting along. You two are working it out;
that's great!" These types of comments can set you up for more
fighting and, like any praise, can backfire. The children may see
it as an attempt to manipulate them.

School

Most parents are genuinely concerned about their children's
progress in school. What they often don't realize, though, is that
their worth as parents may be tied up in their children's performance. You see evidence of this on car bumper stickers that
proclaim: My Child's an Honor Student. We wonder whose self-
esteem this message reflects. Also, how does the parents' pride
in the achieving student affect their siblings' self-esteem?

WAYS PARENTS DISCOURAGE CHILDREN'S INTEREST IN SCHOOL

Many parents are too involved in their children's schooling, through monitoring their grades, attempting to make sure they do their homework, and reminding them to take requested items to school. This involvement takes school responsibilities away from the child.

Some parents pay their children for good grades. What message do you think the child is getting from this action? Is the child really interested in learning or in getting the money? Furthermore, if the child is rebellious, the payments will backfire because he will see them as an attempt to force him to comply.

Punishments often don't work, either. Grounding, restricting TV, denying privileges, all serve as red flags to a rebellious child. Such actions just intensify the power contest.

WAYS PARENTS CAN ENCOURAGE CHILDREN'S INTEREST IN SCHOOL

Learning is a team effort between the teacher, child, and parents. Like any team, each "player" has a job to do in order to have a winning team. It's the teacher's job to teach, the student's job to learn, and the parents' job to prepare the child and provide support and encouragement.

If you're a parent of a young child, you're in a good position to help the child get a good start in shaping a healthy attitude toward learning. Reading to the child, taking her on field trips, and expressing an interest in her schoolwork help fashion a healthy attitude that can carry over throughout her schooling.

But there are many things you can do regardless of the age of your child.

1. Provide adequate nutrition. A nutritious diet helps the mind as well as the body.

2.   Build your child's self-esteem. Feeling good about oneself often creates a desire to learn.

3.   Help your child learn responsibility. Chores, permitting the child to do the things he can do for himself, giving choices and allowing him to take the consequences of his decisions, all help the child learn to be responsible.

4.   Become involved in the parents' organization at your school. If your school has a career day, volunteer to talk about your job. Serve on committees to improve the quality of education in your community. Join or start a parent study group where parents can meet to learn positive parenting skills. (See Appendix C.)

You and Your Child's Homework

Keeping in mind that learning is the child's responsibility, avoid overinvolvement in homework. You can provide adequate lighting, a quiet place for the child to work, and support and encouragement.

Some children will monitor themselves with homework issues. They'll set their own schedules and get the job done. Others may need some help in making homework part of their routine. You can give the child a choice of times to do homework. It's best to let each of your children set his or her own time; your chances of cooperation will improve. For example, Don may want to do it before supper, while Jane may prefer after supper.

If there's a TV program a child wants to watch during her study time, she can change the study time that day, or if you have a VCR, she can tape the program.

LEARNING PROBLEMS AND LACK OF
COOPERATION

Problems with school can be the result of a learning disability, in which case the child may need some special help from a tutor. But the trouble can also be purposive. For example, a child can gain your attention through getting poor grades or by not doing homework unless you're constantly involved with him. The child can gain power or revenge through keeping you in a battle over her grades or homework. Or a child can display inadequacy by proclaiming he just doesn't understand or can't do it.

If your child is seeking attention by not performing, it's best not to attend to misbehavior. If he tries to get you to sit with him during homework or to do it for him, express your confidence in him and let him handle it. If he doesn't finish the work, he'll have to deal with the consequences at school.

Remember to comment on his efforts and the things he does well, whether or not they're related to his schoolwork. Emphasize his strengths.

Conflicts over a child's grades and homework can undermine a positive relationship with the child. You know by now that you can't win a power contest. If your child is determined to defeat you, chances are she will. If not, she'll get even with you. About the only thing you can do in this case is to turn over the job of school to the child. Tell her, respectfully, that you can't make her learn, so you're not going to try anymore. Whether she learns is up to her and that you wish her well. Don't try to force her to stick to a homework schedule.

Be prepared for her to get worse before she gets better in her attempt to pull you back into the battle. But if you stick to your decision, most children will begin to turn around because they don't have you as an opponent. You'll be tempted to get back into the fray, but if you do, you'll lose any progress you've made.

Concentrate on building a positive relationship in other areas of your life with your child. Back out of any other power contests and let any consequences do the teaching. Work on winning cooperation by utilizing her strengths and asking for her help. Power-driven children love to help if it promotes their feeling of importance, and helping is a way for a child to use power constructively.

Teachers may try to get you back into the power contest as well; after all, they're frustrated too. Realize, though, that you've been trying to force the child to improve his grades and do his homework; it hasn't worked, and you're bankrupt. The only thing you can do is back off. Support the teacher in whatever he wants to do as long as you feel his actions won't discourage your child further.

Children who display inadequacy need massive doses of encouragement. Encourage any small step they make in their work as well as in any other area. Remember to focus on their strengths. A child may display inadequacy in schoolwork but be confident in other areas of his life.

LYING AND STEALING

Lying and stealing are two forms of behavior that are most disturbing to parents. They feel that unless they promptly put a stop to such behavior, the child will degenerate into a pathological liar or a thief. The moral aspects of these acts often influence a parent to react quite severely to the culprit.

One must realize that most children lie at some time in their childhood. Most children have also taken things that don't belong to them at one time or another. These occasional misdeeds do not make a child a liar or a thief. The most dangerous aspects of lying and stealing are not the actions themselves but the reactions of the parents. Parents who treat their transgressor as a dishonest person stand a good chance of producing one.

As to who owns the problem, it depends on whom the lying or stealing affects. For example, if a child lies to a friend, that problem is between the child and her friend.

Many times parents unintentionally encourage children to lie by using punishment. When the child misbehaves, he may lie to avoid punishment. But when the child is allowed to experience consequences, lying becomes unnecessary.

Lying

Some children lie when the truth is obvious to everyone.

> Kathy asked Mother if she could have some cookies. Because they would spoil Kathy's dinner, Mother denied her request.
> Mother went to her room for a few minutes. When she returned, she saw Kathy watching television, chocolate cookie crumbs obvious around her mouth.
> "I thought I told you not to have cookies!"
> "I didn't," said Kathy.
> "Then why do you have crumbs all over your face?" asked Mother.
> "Oh," said Kathy, quickly wiping the crumbs off her face.
> "I don't like to be lied to. So just for that, no more TV tonight!"

It is obvious that Kathy did not intend to try to keep secrets from her mother. She could have destroyed the evidence. Why would a child lie when the evidence is so apparent? In this case it seems that Kathy has learned that she can gain attention by lying. If she did not "forget" to take care of the evidence, she could not gain the attention.

This problem belongs to Mother because she's the one who's bothered by it. Taking away TV privileges won't really solve the problem; such a reaction just draws attention to it. Let's suppose Mother acted as if Kathy had no crumbs on her face. Suppose she pretended that Kathy did not raid the cookie jar. If Mother did not give Kathy the opportunity to lie, she would gain no attention from "cookie crumbs on the face" behavior. After a few tries Kathy would probably take no for an answer.

Some children may use behavior such as Kathy's for the purpose of power or revenge. In these cases the parents may have to lock things up while refraining from playing detective and punishing.

In some situations lying cannot be ignored.

> Eight-year-old Brad told his dad he was going to Jim's house. At about four o'clock Dad called Jim's mother, Mrs. Jordan, to ask her to send Brad home. Mrs. Jordan said that Brad was not there and hadn't been at her house or playing with Jim all day.
>
> In a few minutes Brad came home. "Where have you been?" demanded Dad.
>
> "At Jim's," Brad replied nervously.
>
> "Don't you lie to me! I just called Mrs. Jordan and she said you haven't been there all day. Now, where were you?"

Dad owns this problem because he's naturally concerned about Brad's safety and, of course, his whereabouts. But Dad's decision to give Brad the third degree is no guarantee that he will get a truthful answer or that Brad won't lie in the future. In fact, Dad's action may increase Brad's lying. It appears that Brad has decided to show his dad by his lies that he intends to do only what he wants to do. Dad is determined to prove that he can't, and thus we have a power contest. Suppose Dad had handled the situation like this:

> When Brad came home, Dad made no comment about where he had actually gone. However, the next day, when Brad approached Dad to tell him he was going someplace, Dad said, "I'm sorry, Brad, but yesterday you didn't go to Jim's as you had said you would. Therefore, you'll have to stay home today, and tomorrow we'll see if you are ready to go out on your own."

With this approach, Dad has kept his control. He has been firm but kind, without accusing or moralizing. And he has offered Brad another chance to prove his trustworthiness. His chances of influencing Brad are much greater.

It was a nice sunny day and Mr. and Mrs. Ellis were out in the backyard doing some gardening. Judy, ten, and Greg, nine, were in the house. Suddenly, the Ellises heard a crash. Mr. Ellis went into the house to see what had happened and found a broken lamp. Mr. Ellis asked the children, "What happened to the lamp?"

Judy answered, "I don't know. Greg must have broken it."

"I didn't."

"You did, too."

The children continued to argue, each proclaiming his own innocence and accusing the other. Mr. Ellis interrupted them: "I'm sorry, but I have no way of knowing who did this, so you'll both have to pay for it out of your allowance."

Both children complained bitterly, but Mr. Ellis didn't argue. "Now, how shall we arrange payment? The lamp cost forty dollars. How much do each of you wish to pay out of your weekly allowances?" The children still complained, but Mr. Ellis went on as if they were not complaining, proposing ways they could pay for it. Finally, the children calmed down and made arrangements to pay.

The children own this problem because one of them broke the lamp. While holding them both responsible may seem unfair to the innocent one, Mr. Ellis had no alternative; he had no way of knowing who broke the lamp. Since the children could not get Dad to play detective or to take sides, they finally settled down and took the consequences.

Some children's lies take the form of exaggeration or tall tales.

Sandy, eleven, would often irritate her parents by exaggerating and stretching the truth. They would usually respond to her proclamations with such comments as "You know that's not true" or "Oh, come on, who do you think you're kidding?" Sandy would then elaborately defend her statements. The session normally ended with resentment and the continuance of a poor relationship.

What Sandy's parents don't realize is that her exaggerations are symptoms of a deeper discouragement. It appears that Sandy doesn't feel she can gain a place through useful contributions, so she gains the attention and recognition she desires through useless tales.

While Sandy owns this problem, her parents will want to help her find a way to solve her problem. They can begin by avoiding reinforcing her misbehavior. They simply can listen, refraining from negative comment or nonverbal cues, when she decides to exaggerate. Facial expression will be of the utmost importance. If her parents show through their body language that they disapprove of Sandy, they will be reinforcing the behavior.

If silence isn't effective, Sandy's parents could help her understand her purpose by reflecting: "It seems that you feel it's important to impress us." If a discussion follows, the parents can employ their reflective-listening skills and help Sandy reconsider the importance of being overconcerned with impressing others. They can help her explore the possibility of recognition for positive contributions and then find ways for Sandy to establish a place by being useful. They can begin by capitalizing on her best contributions to the family.

Stealing

How a parent reacts when a child steals often helps to determine the child's view of himself as an honest or dishonest person.

While cleaning seven-year-old Mike's room, Brenda discovered a baseball glove that she knew wasn't his. She approached Mike with "Where did you get this glove?"

"I borrowed it from Tommy."

Brenda could tell from Mike's facial expression that "borrow" wasn't the proper word.

"You mean you stole it, don't you?" asked Brenda angrily.

Mike hung his head and didn't answer.

"Now, listen here, you know stealing is very wrong. You just march down to Tommy's and give it back to him right now!"

While Brenda may have been successful in forcing Mike to return the glove, her action didn't help her relationship with her son. Lecturing and defining him as a thief certainly generated resentment and doesn't guarantee that he will not repeat the behavior in the future.

Let's suppose Brenda had used a different approach.

When Mike said that he had borrowed the baseball glove she discovered, Brenda replied, "I guess you'll have to take it back to him. He'll probably be needing it."

Brenda refrained from playing detective. She acted as if she believed Mike and simply suggested he return the glove. There was no need for Mike to become defensive and resentful, since Brenda handled the situation in a friendly manner. There was no need to lecture Mike on the evils of stealing; he knows stealing is wrong. Since he received no reinforcement for his misbehavior, Mike will probably stop "borrowing."

Burt noticed that some of his change was missing from his dresser top. He asked other family members if they knew what had happened to it. Everyone denied knowledge of its whereabouts.

The next day, while preparing the clothes for washing, Burt found some loose change in ten-year-old Bob's pocket. On questioning him about the money, he announced that he had found it on the school playground.

"I don't believe you, Bob. This is just about the same amount that I'm missing. You stole this from me, didn't you?"

"Yes," replied Bob nervously.

"What did you do with the rest of it?"

"I bought some candy."

Burt spanked Bob, declaring that he wouldn't have a thief in his house.

Burt's punishing and name-calling are discouraging and almost guarantee resentment and possible retaliation from Bob.

Let's see what might have happened if the situation had been handled differently.

... The next day, Burt found some loose change in ten-year-old Bob's pocket. Burt approached Bob. "Bob, it appears that you have my missing change. If you feel you need more money, we can discuss a raise in your allowance or a plan for you to earn some extra money, but right now I'd like to have my change back. Also, we have to discuss how you will pay back the money you spent."

Here Bob's dad has approached the problem in a more positive way, and his chances of influencing Bob are much greater. He has refused to punish and lecture. Instead, he has offered his son a chance to discuss how he can honestly obtain more money, at the same time making his son responsible for returning all the money he took.

But suppose you're missing something and don't know who took it. What then? Tell your children what's missing and set a time and place for the property to be returned. No one need know who took it. If it's not returned, hold all the children accountable and let them figure out how they will return or replace the item.[3]

Suppose your child takes something from a store. Consider the example of Mr. and Mrs. Carson.

Mr. and Mrs. Carson and their three children went to the mall. While in the department store, eleven-year-old June said she wanted to look around in the girls' clothing department. The parents agreed, telling June to meet them at the snack bar for lunch in about fifteen minutes.

Two days later, Mrs. Carson was looking for a pair of June's slacks that needed mending. She happened to see a blouse in June's closet that had never been there before. Then she remembered how extremely quiet June had been at lunch and on the way home after the trip to the mall. And she remembered how anxious to get to her room June had been.

"June," said Mother, "where did you get this blouse?"

June's face reddened. "I bought it at the store the other day."

"I'm sorry, June, but I know how much this blouse costs, and you didn't have the money. What do you think should be done about this?"

June shrugged her shoulders and made no reply.

Mrs. Carson said, "I think this is really between you and the store manager, so we'll go back to the store, and you can talk to him about it."

Mrs. Carson approached a difficult problem in a positive way. It is probable that experiencing the embarrassment of facing the store manager will help June learn from her mistake.

Sometimes older children and teens will become involved with the police. Let them experience the consequences provided by law.[4]

If lying or stealing become severe or persistent, seek the counsel of a professional, as they may be symptoms of a more serious difficulty, such as stealing to buy drugs.

PEER RELATIONSHIPS

When a child has difficulty making friends or getting along with peers, parents naturally become concerned. What parents don't realize is that the child must learn on his own how to get along with others. Parental interference in the child's peer relationships often only makes the situation worse.

Perhaps the most destructive response is feeling sorry for the child who exhibits difficulty in the social-relations area. Pity allows the child to feel that he is incapable of handling the situation, and he easily convinces himself that there is nothing to do about the problem except join his parents in feeling sorry. Children who have peer-relationship problems, like all other discouraged children, need encouragement, not pity.

If your child is upset about a relationship with a friend, listen to his feelings and help him explore alternatives for solving the problem. The only exception to this is bullying. If your child is being bullied and you believe the child will get hurt, you'll need to step in. If your child is a bully, seek professional help.

BAD INFLUENCES

Parents who are concerned with "bad" influences often create battlegrounds over their child's choice of friends. Overconcern and attempts to prevent a child from playing with whom he chooses often increase the child's desire to associate with such companions. In addition, trying to select a child's friends denies him necessary experiences, for children must learn to deal with all kinds of people.

Your best assurance that your child will choose positive friendships is your own relationship with him. If you have a strong relationship and have communicated your values effectively, chances are your children will choose friends with similar values.

You can discuss with your child how people go about choosing friends. A friend is someone

- who has values similar to yours;
- who likes the same things you do;
- with whom you feel safe sharing personal beliefs and feelings;
- you can count on;
- you can trust.[5]

Get to know the children your child chooses as friends; if possible, get to know their parents as well. Of course, knowing parents as your child matures becomes more of a challenge, but you can insist that you meet the child's friends. Also, make sure you know where your child is and if there is supervision.

If you have concerns about a child's friend, ask the child, "What is there about _____ that you like?" If you find his answers disturbing, discuss your concerns. "I'm worried about your association with _____ because . . ."

If you're convinced that association with a certain child can create problems for your child, such as involvement in drugs or sex, attempt to terminate the relationship. Realize, though, how challenging this is. Give logical reasons for your decision. Listen to the child's feelings but stick to your action. Tell the child you'll expect her to follow your wishes or you'll have to give close supervision to her activities that will restrict her freedom.[6]

PEER PRESSURE

Parents of teens and preteens worry about losing their influence to their child's peer group. While it's true that the child's peers do influence him, parents have more influence than they think. If your relationship is based on mutual respect and trust, if you accept your teen as a budding adult, if you respect their desire for independence, your influence will be positive. But if you insist on controlling their lives, treat them like children, or try to keep them on a short leash, you'll be asking for trouble. Does this mean that you should let them do as they please? Of course not! Permissiveness is an abandonment of parental responsibility. It teaches teens that they have a right to do whatever they want. This is an unrealistic picture of life; even adults don't get to do everything they want. There are rules that teens need to follow. It is hoped that through the family meeting your teens have participated in establishing some of the rules.

DATING[7]

At what age should teens date? Whom should they date? Where should they be allowed to go? When should they be home? What about sex? These questions plague many parents of teens. The age of dating depends on when your teen is ready. If you think your teen is too young, consider his purpose. Are his friends dating and does he want to gain their approval? Is this becoming a power issue between the two of you? You certainly have the right to say no, but realize that he won't let you off easily. Give reasons for your denial. Be prepared to listen.

If you think your teen is of an age where she should date but she's not, consider the reasons. Remember, not all people are ready for experiences at the same time. She may have trouble with relationships; she may need some counseling. It could also be a power issue between the two of you. If you think this is the case, back out of the contest and trust her to date when she's ready.

If you think your son or daughter is wanting to date the wrong person, consider the reasons for your opinion. What is it about the person that concerns you? Does it involve your own prejudices? Do you think there's too much of an age difference? Do you worry about the other teen's influence on your teenager? If you worry about age differences or influence, you can decide to trust your teen or attempt to terminate the relationship.

When your teen is to be home after a date relates to any other curfew issue. Discuss it with your teen. Negotiate a time and a phone call if he'll be late. Logical consequences of not going out the next time prevail if your teen violates the agreement.

What about sex? Later in this chapter we'll discuss this topic. After you've discussed it with your teen, it really boils down to trust, like so many other issues with teenagers.

GANGS

Authors Jane Nelsen, Lynn Lott, and H. Stephen Glenn point out that children (including those younger than teens) join gangs because they want to belong, feel powerful, and feel safe.[8]

If you satisfy these three wants in your relationship with your teen, his desire to join a gang will diminish. Teens feel they belong when they are respected, encouraged, and have an opportunity to contribute. Being permitted to make decisions (within limits, of course) gives them a sense of power. Safety is more challenging. If you live in a relatively safe community, it may not be a problem. Common sense will prevail. Discuss with your child how to be safe and what to do if he feels threatened or is uncomfortable in a neighborhood or situation. Discuss; don't preach! Get his ideas; give yours. Develop a plan together.

If you live in a neighborhood with a strong gang influence, consider moving.[9] If, for some reason, that isn't possible, gang-proof your child as best you can. There may be youth groups your child can join at school or at your church that are not gang affiliated. Many neighborhoods are forming parent groups to counteract gangs. Consider joining or starting such a group. In the final analysis, if gangs become a problem, it's time to seek help.

SEX

Children today are surrounded by sexuality. They see it on TV and in films. Even some films labeled "PG" allude to sex. Some TV commercials exude sexuality. They teach children that women, and sometimes men, have to be sexy to attract the other sex. As a parent, you can control some of the things your children see on TV and in films. You can't control all of it. But you can use the media as springboards for discussion if your children are old enough to benefit by it. "What does that commercial say about men and women?" "Why do you think the woman is wearing such clothing?"

Your own comfort level on this subject will influence how you deal with it. Can you discuss it openly? Is it a taboo subject for you? Examine your attitudes. Be realistic, for sex is a part of life. It won't go away because you're uncomfortable discussing it.

Parents often wonder when to start teaching about sex. Sex education is a gradual process, beginning in early childhood.

> "Mommy, where did I come from?" asks wide-eyed six-year-old Brad.
>
> "Well, ah, you see, Brad, when a mommy and daddy really love each other, the man puts his . . . *[Twenty minutes later.]* Does that answer your question?"
>
> "Ah, well, Tina said she was from Cleveland; I just wondered where I was from."

This old joke illustrates the point that answering young children's questions about sex doesn't have to be a technical explanation of the mechanics. Young children, even infants, are intrigued by their bodies. As they become a little older, about two and a half to four, they become curious about other children's bodies, their own sex, and the other sex. They will ask questions. Your answers can be general and age appropriate.[10] Your local library or bookstore will have books for various age groups about sex. Choose those that conform with your values. Make reading them to, or with, children part of your time together.

Their curiosity may lead to exploration or "playing doctor" with other children. If you discover such activity, talk with your child. Acknowledge his or her interest, answer questions, but let the child know that the behavior is inappropriate. Don't preach or punish. Just be matter-of-fact about it. "This is something we don't do. If you have questions, I'll be glad to answer them." Keep a close eye on such relationships.[11] If you find the child engaged in sexual play, simply separate him or her from the other child without comment.

As they grow, children gradually expand their knowledge about sex. Besides the mechanics, they discuss attitudes, values, and love. We can be too concerned about sexual intercourse and too little concerned about social intercourse.

There's more to sex education than sex. Teaching children to act responsibly helps them make appropriate decisions about sex. Throughout this book we've talked about how to help children make good decisions. Teaching children how to make friends also plays a part in the crowd they'll choose to hang with when they're older. (See "Peer Relationships.")

MASTURBATION

Most children masturbate. It's not bad, unnatural, or unhealthy. If you have religious values that prohibit such activity, share your values with your child. At the same time, realize that trying to make the child feel guilty will probably lead to more of what you don't want. A power contest can develop.

If masturbation is excessive, it may be a sign of boredom or lack of affection. Help your child become involved in healthy activities and make sure you demonstrate your love and affection. Some children may need counseling if the problem persists.

PRETEENS AND TEENS

As children approach puberty, sexual interest heightens. If you've been discussing sexuality and teaching your values since your children were young, the transition will be smoother. They will have some idea about where you stand and will have developed some attitudes of their own. If your children have developed different attitudes, listen and give your own ideas and the reasons for them.

Discuss the consequences of sexual involvement in a frank, nonpreachy manner. Of course, you'll want to talk about AIDS and other sexually transmitted diseases (STDs) and pregnancy, but your discussion needs to go beyond that. Focus on emotional consequences, the pressure to have sex, and how pregnancy can radically affect a young person's life. What will happen to his or her life? What about plans for the future? Share your own concerns and fears about disease and the child's future.

Discuss the positive benefits of abstinence. Obviously they won't be exposed to disease, and pregnancy won't be a possibility, but that's what won't happen. Talk about what can happen. They will be fully giving themselves to their chosen marital partner. Entering marriage as a virgin is a sign of real responsibility and commitment. Currently there is a movement among teens to postpone sex, and for those who've been sexually active, a "second virginity" program.[12]

But suppose you suspect that your child may become sexually active despite your best efforts. What then? Of course, your beliefs about contraception will influence your actions. This decision is not easy if one has strong religious feelings on the subject.

Realize that sex, like any human behavior, involves choice and serves a purpose. Yes, sex is a drive, but the individual is in the driver's seat! Consider certain religious groups whose clerics choose to remain celibate.

The obvious purpose of sex is pleasure, but there are others. A desire for intimacy, love, companionship, and peer recognition can all come into play. Sex can be used as a weapon against parents—for power or revenge. Sex can fulfill a drive for excitement. Once you realize the purposes sex can fulfill, you will be in a position to see if you can help your child fulfill those purposes in other ways.

AIDS AND OTHER STDS

AIDS and other STDs are naturally frightening to parents. When you talk to your child about sex, be sure to discuss STDs. Many books on children/teens and sex contain information about disease. A trip to the library or bookstore can acquaint you with the facts. Also, many communities have AIDS information services—check your local phone book. Your public health department will also have information. And there's the CDC National HIV and AIDS hotline at (1-800) 342-2437. (An 800 number can sometimes change. If you find any 800 number given in this book nonfunctional, you can find the new number by calling the toll-free directory at [1-800] 555-1212.) Once you're aware of the facts, it's time to talk with your teen. First, ask him what he knows about the disease. Listen to what he has to say; he may have misconceptions or he may know more than you think. Share the information you've learned. Show him the material from which you obtained your information. He may want to read it for himself. If he challenges you or the material you're using, don't become defensive. Encourage him to find his own literature and discuss it with you. Suggest places he can obtain information, such as the CDC National HIV and AIDS hotline. Like any talk with teens, keep it friendly and listen. Remember that lecturing isn't going to help; you're simply exchanging information. Realize, too, that many teens feel invincible: "It won't happen to me." You can't force your teen to accept the information; all you can do is share. Note that any resistance may be just a way of testing you—seeing if he can push your buttons.

PREGNANCY[13]

Oscar C. Christensen talks about "purposeful pregnancy." Both boys and girls can use it as a means of achieving status—how many babies they can produce. Girls can use pregnancy to gain someone to love who won't be critical or to leave home and gain independence by going on welfare. Unrealistic attitudes for sure, but purposes nonetheless.

Purposeful pregnancy can involve a show of power or to get even with parents. A power contest may develop around the issue of sexuality. So the girl uses the ultimate weapon, getting pregnant. This defeats the parents and hurts their feelings as well.

If your daughter is pregnant, your shock and anger may lead to rejection. But this is when your daughter really needs you. Listen to her feelings.

If possible, meet with the boy and his parents. Discuss options. The problem belongs to your daughter and possibly the father. Everyone's feelings about abortion and early marriage will come into play. It may be best to seek professional guidance as you and your daughter work through this problem.

If your son is a father, discuss his feelings and intentions. Use your listening skills. Explore how he can accept his responsibility. There are teen fathers who want to be included in decisions about pregnancy. Realize that legal issues are developing concerning a father's rights and custody. There have been court cases awarding former teen fathers custody years after the child's birth.

DRUGS

When children take drugs, the parent obviously owns the problem. Why do they take drugs? We live in a drug-filled society; both legal and illegal drugs surround us. Count the number of TV commercials in any one day to see how many times there's an advertisement for drugs. Got a headache? Take this pill. Got a backache? Take this one. Sleeping problems? Here's how to fix that. While there are times when such drugs are necessary, you need to examine your own drug-taking habits. Do you run to the medicine cabinet every time you have an ache? What kind of message is this giving your children?

Then there's alcohol, tobacco, and caffeine. Examine your

habits around these substances. Do you drink? Smoke? Have to have a cup of coffee to wake up in the morning?

While over-the-counter drugs, alcohol, tobacco, and caffeine are all legal substances, they still send a message to children about drug use.

Then there are illegal drugs. They're easy to get despite law enforcement efforts. And drugs that are legal for adults but illegal for children—like alcohol—are also easy to get. What parents don't realize is that alcohol is still the most used and abused drug by children and teens.

Besides the models of drug use, children can gain a sense of power through using drugs. They know that their parents don't want them to take drugs, so they can defeat the parents by doing so. They can also get revenge by putting their own lives in danger.

Curiosity and peer acceptance also motivate children; if their friends are into it, they want to fit in. A sense of excitement can also motivate them. It's exciting to violate the law. And some drugs create a sense of excitement on their own. A child can also use drugs to escape life—a form of display of inadequacy.

Helping Your Child Stay Drug-Free[14]

While there's no absolute guarantee that your children won't become involved in drugs, there are some things you can do to influence them.

Children who get on drugs lack self-esteem and decision-making skills and are too dependent on peer approval. If you concentrate on encouragement and valuing your child, you will help build his or her self-esteem. Focus on the child's strengths and interests. Offering choices and allowing the child to experience the consequences of the decisions—positive or negative—helps build decision-making abilities. Exploring alternatives and regular family meetings also increase decision-making skills and give children a sense of contribution.

If you have a good relationship with your children based on

mutual respect and acceptance, they won't be overpowered by the desire for peer acceptance. Children overconcerned with peer acceptance want badly to belong, which often means that they don't have a sense of belonging in the family. Even parents of teens have more influence over their teens than they think. You want to make sure that the influence is of a positive nature.

Give them accurate drug information. Again, don't preach; just share. Listen to their comments and questions about drugs. Discuss why people take them. If you have young children, don't wait until they're of an age to be interested in drugs. Just as you inform them about safety and strangers, teach them about drugs. Use information appropriate to their age level. As they grow, add more information. Keep up-to-date yourself. Your local police department will have such information. Also check the local Yellow Pages on "Alcoholism and Drug Abuse" and "Treatment Centers." A national source for publications and locating treatment centers in your area is the National Clearing House for Alcohol and Drug Abuse, 11426-28 Rockville Pike, Suite 200, Rockville, MD 20852 ([1-800] 662-4357).

Know what's going on in your community. Keep up with the news. Go to any public lectures on the topic.

Healthy, positive family activities give children a sense of well-being. Family exercise periods are a good example. Your valuing exercise gives children a healthy role model. Also, encourage them to engage in healthy peer activities, whether through after-school programs, church, Little League, or boy-girl organizations like the Scouts.

Teaching Your Child to Say No

Television commercials selling pain relievers and beer are good springboards for discussion. Ask your children what point the manufacturer is trying to get across. In the case of medication, what nonmedical options are available for common complaints like headaches? As for beer commercials, discuss why people drink and what the commercial is trying to say. This beer tastes better than others? It's "cool" to drink beer? Real men drink beer? Women who drink beer are sexy?

TV programs that involve drug use are also good discussion starters. How did the character begin to take drugs? What was he or she getting out of it? What were the consequences? What was missing in the character's life? How could the person solve his or her problems without drugs?

Use "what if" scenarios to get the children to consider what they would do. For example, what if a friend tried to get them to drink or take other drugs or hold illegal substances for them? If your child doesn't know what he or she would do, you could take the what if to another level. "What if you did this? What might happen?"

What Can I Do If I Suspect My Child Is Taking Drugs?

Seek professional help. You can't handle the problem by yourself. Your family doctor may know of a referral source. If not, the National Clearing House mentioned above can guide you to agencies in your area. Local phone books also list drug-treatment agencies.

VIOLENCE

Marsha's sons, six-year-old Sam and four-year-old Tom, were arguing. Sam popped Tom in the nose, and Tom immediately let out a wail. Marsha ran to the scene, assessed what had happened, grabbed Sam, and smacked him firmly on the bottom, saying, "We don't hit people!"

Ironic? Yes. Marsha's trying to stop hitting by hitting! It's not going to work. Many parents spank at times, out of frustration mostly, not knowing what else to do. But spanking, regardless of the misbehavior problem, only teaches children violent approaches to problem solving. And we have enough problems with violence in this world. So if you're concerned about violence in our society, the first thing you need to do is to resolve never to hit your children. Don't even use it as a last resort. You know about last resorts; you'll resort to them. Spanking needs to be off your list of options along with name-calling and threats that damage self-esteem. You can seek other, nonviolent solutions to misbehavior of any kind. (If you find yourself frequently and/or severely hitting your children, or if your spouse or another adult is abusing your children, *seek help immediately*.)

You can influence your children to be nonviolent by:

- Telling your children that you love them and expressing affection. Open telling and touching children show them that they are loved and valued. If you're married, demonstrate affection between you and your spouse. Open expression of affection between adults and children and adults and adults models loving relationships between people.
- Having fun together. Playing games, laughing, going on outings help build a strong family unit whose members care about one another.
- Exploring alternatives. This skill models peaceful problem solving. Reflective listening "hears" children's feelings, and I-messages help you convey your feelings in nonthreatening ways. Brainstorming allows everyone to participate in seeking solutions.
- Being encouraging. Encouragement builds self-esteem. Children with high self-esteem have mutual respect and care about others.
- Using natural and logical consequences. These disciplinary methods are peaceful ways to solve conflicts. Children learn to take responsibility for their choices.

Many parents are concerned about the violence shown on TV, in movies, and in computer games. You can restrict the TV programs and films your children see and the computer games purchased or "downloaded" from modems.

You can also watch some violent TV programs together and

discuss them. Was violence used just to make a film exciting? Was it necessary to the story? Realize that not all violent shows are bad; some of them have a message. For example, violent people are brought to justice—the consequence of being violent. If it's a war story, wars are violent and a failure to find peaceful solutions. Ask your children for their opinions about the program. Use your reflective-listening skills to demonstrate that you understand their feelings and beliefs. Express your own feelings and opinions. Ask them what they think could have been done in the story to bring about a peaceful solution. Avoid preaching; just listen and share ideas.

Realize that one of the most violent shows on TV is the news. Watching the news together is another way to discuss violence and other solutions.

Finally, watch what you say when you're angry—with your children or with others. Violent and hate talk have an influence on children. Children learn from models, and parents are major models for children.

SINGLE, MARRIED, REMARRIED: APPLYING YOUR SKILLS TO YOUR FAMILY STRUCTURE

>-+-+>-O-+>-+-<

T HE SKILLS YOU'VE learned in this book apply to any family—single-parent family, stepfamily, or original two-parent family. There are unique challenges in single families and stepfamilies that we'll discuss later in this chapter. Let's begin by discussing original two-parent, or "nuclear," families.

THE NUCLEAR FAMILY—THE IDEAL SITUATION?

Society assumes that nuclear families are always best for raising children. Problems of two-parent families are often ignored as we point fingers at single parents for the ills of society. Taking a closer look, however, we find that two-parent families are not always as ideal as they seem. The ideal nuclear family would be two parents who have a good relationship and are mostly in agreement on how to raise their children. However, this is not always the case; in fact, it seldom ever is.

Parents don't always agree: disagreements about raising children are quite common. Why? Because people come from different backgrounds and have different expectations. Minor disagreements are not that serious and often lead to compromise. But when parents have major disagreements, severe conflict is often the result.

George was raised in a strict home. His father ruled the roost with a strong hand; physical punishment was common. George felt that he turned out all right and that his father's way was the best way to raise children.

Margaret, on the other hand, was raised in a permissive home in which most behaviors were tolerated and her parents never lifted a hand against their children. She believes that love is all children need and they'll turn out all right.

Needless to say, there was much conflict over how to raise the children. George would threaten, restrict, and spank. Margaret would feel sorry for the children and let them get away with murder. George and Margaret argued constantly about how to treat the children, and the children played the adults off against each other.

Is this a good situation for the children? Will they survive it? Being resilient, most children will survive such a conflict, but what are they learning? It's a good bet that they'll become master manipulators and carry that "skill" into their adult relationships.

When parents have major disagreements, they have three choices. They can do nothing, agree to disagree, or divorce.

The first choice is very common and the most detrimental to the children. In fact, it often leads to the third one—divorce. The second choice can work. Each parent agrees to handle his or her relationship with the children in his or her own way and not to interfere with the spouse's relationship (child abuse excepted, of course). The children learn their limits with each parent. This is not all bad; children have to learn how to deal with all kinds of people as they grow toward adulthood.

The third choice can be beneficial to the children as well. The popular attitude that divorce damages children discounts children's ability to adapt to situations they find themselves in, with divorce no exception. Children aren't weak. The damaging effects of divorce are more the result of society's attitudes about it than the actual divorce. Which is better for children, constant parental conflict or the love and support of a strong single parent? But we don't want to minimize divorce's impact on children; it's an adjustment, and it can be long-term.

Of course, when parents have serious disagreements, it's best that they seek counseling. A competent counselor can help them sort out their differences and make decisions on how they want to handle their disagreements. Your family doctor, minister, a teacher or school counselor, or a friend who's had counseling can often suggest a good marriage and family counselor.

We've mentioned the effects of divorce briefly; in the following section we'll take a closer look at divorce and its effects on parents and children.

DIVORCE DOESN'T HAVE TO BE DESTRUCTIVE

Divorce is a fact of life in modern society. (In fact, the divorce rate in the United States is around 50 percent!) No one would deny that divorce is traumatic for children—and for adults as well. But divorce doesn't have to be a death sentence for self-esteem for parents or children. Strong single-parent families, like any strong family, can raise encouraged and cooperative children.

Divorce and Guilt

The trauma for people involved in divorce is increased when parents feel guilty about the divorce. Many parents feel they've failed when they divorce and have damaged their children. They fail to see that the divorce may have been the best choice they could make under the circumstances. (For a full discussion of guilt feelings, see chapter 4 on emotions.) Failure is not really the issue; a decision that's best for everyone involved is usually the case. As we've said, children are resilient. They can stand the change in their family structure, although they usually don't like it.

The children often feel guilty as well. They may think, If I'd just been better, this wouldn't have happened; it's my fault. You need to do your best to assure your children that the divorce isn't the result of their actions. You might say, "Sometimes adults find they just can't get along and it's best to divorce. It really has nothing to do with you. There's nothing you could've done to make things any different." Then listen and hear their feelings. You may have to do this several times, especially in preparing children for separation and the early stages of the divorce.

Divorce and Pity

One of the strongest effects of divorce on the children is not the event itself but the attitude of the adults involved. Parents, grandparents, close relatives, and friends often feel sorry for the children. This pity communicates to the children that they can't handle it. Many children "buy into" the assumption of the adults. They may act out or display inadequacy as a result.

If you have firm resolve and really believe you've done what's best and that your children will survive, you, and the children, will be in the best position to cope with the new situation. Talk to your relatives and friends; let them know what you and the children need from them—faith, not pity.

Tom was the father of two children, eight and six. He and his wife, Tanya, had decided to divorce. Tom informed his parents. Tom's mother said, "Poor Jill and Tommy, divorce is such a horrible thing. Can't you and Tanya work this out, Tom?"

"We've tried, Mom; been to counseling for several months. This just seems to be the best for all of us."

"But I feel so sorry for the children," Mom said.

"Mom, I understand that you're concerned, but the

children and I really need your support on this."

"What do you mean, Tom? You know you have our support," his dad replied.

"I know that, Dad. It's just that I think if we feel sorry for Jill and Tommy, we'll give them the idea that they can't handle this."

"Well, divorce is rough on children, son," said Dad.

"I know, it's rough on all of us, but if we all have faith in their ability to handle it—tough as it is—I think we'll get through it better."

Tom has communicated his concern and desires to his parents. He has no guarantee that they will follow his wishes and may have to talk to them again several times. If he finds he just can't get through, he may have to put his feelings in stronger terms; they can see the children only if they are willing to change their attitude toward them. This is drastic for most, but it's necessary to preserve the children's self-esteem. Your parents will come around; they will want to see their grandchildren.

Divorce and Grief

Divorce is the death of a relationship. As in any death, there's often grief involved. In 1969 physician Elisabeth Kübler-Ross published her landmark book *On Death and Dying*.[1] In it, she outlined five stages of grief. We find that these stages apply to divorce as well as actual physical death. It's important to understand the stages and that everyone will go through them in his or her individual way and pace.[2]

1. Denial. In this first stage, the family denies that the divorce is actually happening. They aren't willing to accept the facts and often panic.
2. Anger. The second stage often involves a lot of anger. The spouses are angry at each other. The children may be angry at the absent family member, believing she or

he deserted them. Or they may be angry at the custodial parent, believing the parent drove the absent parent away; or they could be angry at both. The children may also be angry with themselves, believing they caused the divorce.

3. Bargaining. Here members try to delay the inevitable. They believe things will be better if there's a second chance: "I'll change, I promise. I won't ever do that again."

4. Depression. Members are depressed about what has happened. Their self-anger and sense of responsibility for the divorce leads to depression. They may see the situation as hopeless. Learning to cope with this temporary depression paves the way for the final stage, acceptance.

5. Acceptance. Members, in their own way and at their own pace, have come to terms with the divorce. They've developed hope and can see possibilities. They are ready to get on with life.

Your recognition of these stages can help you and your children come to terms with the divorce. Remember that it's natural to grieve for a lost relationship and that this grief affects both the adults and the children in the family.

Divorce and Stress

Any life change has the potential for stress. Anger, anxiety, grief, and depression all contribute to the stress you and your children will experience due to divorce. Learning to manage your feelings and help your children manage theirs will reduce the stress. The information in chapter 4 about emotions will help you through the stressful time. Here's a brief review of ways to handle stress:

1. Learn to relax. Deep breathing and muscle relaxation calm you. You can also teach these skills to your children.

2. Exercise. Physical exercise calms you and energizes you at the same time. Set up regular exercise periods. If your children are inactive, encourage them to exercise, too. Some families set up family exercise periods: walking, bicycling, going to health clubs.

3. Watch your self-talk. What you say to yourself influences your feelings. Are you "catastrophizing," placing demands on yourself and others, berating yourself or others, proclaiming your helplessness? "I can't stand it!" Decide to change your self-talk. Listen to what your children believe as well. Help them see how they're upsetting themselves.

4. Take some time for yourself. Being a parent results in a busy life; being a single parent can produce even a busier one. You need to take time out. See your friends; engage in activities you enjoy. Encourage your children to do the same. It's important to make this time part of your weekly schedule or you'll be tempted to ignore it when things pile up.

SETTLING YOUR DIFFERENCES WITH YOUR EX-SPOUSE IN PRIVATE

Your differences with your spouse are yours, not the children's. Arguing in front of children can only increase their grief and stress. The same is true of involving them in your disagreements by expecting them to take sides. It's extremely stressful for a child to think that the only way to get your love is to be disloyal to the other parent.

Keeping your disagreements private also means not giving press releases to your children about what you and your ex are arguing about. It's none of their business. Doing so will only invite the children to manipulate the relationship.

Hard as it is, keep judgments out of your communication with your ex. It's challenging to not judge when you feel hurt, angry, or cheated. But remember: "Today's judge may be tomorrow's defendant."[3] Use the communication skills you've learned in this book to discuss issues with your ex. Reflective listening, I-messages, and exploring alternatives are skills that can help you resolve differences.

Issues of custody are often the source of conflict in divorce relationships. The next section will discuss custody.

CUSTODY

Custody is a crucial challenge of divorce. The custodial arrangement you make with your ex must reflect what is in the best interests of the children.

Of course, the courts can help make custodial arrangements, but you're better off if you can work it out with a counselor. Choose a counselor who has experience with divorcing couples and agrees to help you make the arrangements. Sometimes your friends or your minister will know someone to recommend. Make sure that the children are included in at least one of the counseling sessions so that they can be heard and their feelings considered.[4]

While counseling can help you work out mutually acceptable agreements, especially where the children are concerned, you'll still need a lawyer to act in your best interests with the courts. When you go to court, be clear as to what you want. The court's decision binds all parties. With extremely crowded calendars, judges aren't very amenable to making changes that could've been worked out in the original agreement with sufficient thought and time invested in settling your disputes in the first place. Of course, things can come up that weren't anticipated, but for the most part, be prepared before you ask the court to approve the terms of your divorce.

Custody Arrangements

Be aware that there is no ideal custody arrangement, sole or joint; each has its advantages and disadvantages. Sole custody is traditional, but there is a movement toward joint custody if the parents are willing to cooperate as coparents. Sole custody provides consistency in the relationship between parent and children, but it also puts the most burden on one parent. Joint custody divides the responsibility but requires the highest degree of cooperation, which can be very challenging when hurt feelings and strong differences of opinion exist.

Sole Custody

With sole custody, the children's main residence is with one parent. The noncustodial parent may have visitation rights, but the primary rights and responsibilities for parenthood rest with the custodial parent. Sole custody is still awarded mostly to mothers, but fathers are increasingly seeking this arrangement.[5]

Whether Mom or Dad gets sole custody, its award may not be rewarding. As we mentioned above, with this arrangement the major load is on the custodial parent. In addition to this, sole custody can be the result of the divorcing parents' unwillingness to cooperate for the sake of the children. In this case, the children become pawns in the relationship—hardly in their best interests.

Sometimes sole custody is awarded because one of the parents is judged unfit. But at other times it can be an agreement between spouses. Suppose the mother wants to go to college in another city and doesn't want to uproot the children. The father may agree to take sole custody until the mother finishes her studies. At the conclusion of her training, other arrangements could be made, such as joint custody.

Joint Custody

Does this mean joint custody is better than sole custody? Not necessarily. Again it's back to what is in the best interests of the children. If parents are willing to work hard at coparenting and the arrangement doesn't unduly disrupt the children's lives, then joint custody can be the best arrangement. It requires a lot of discussions and decisions and a commitment of time to work things out, but if you and your ex are willing to make the effort, then joint custody might be possible.

Noncustodial Parents

In sole custodial arrangements, there is naturally a noncustodial parent. If you are a noncustodial parent, your parenting rights may be limited, but you aren't a nonparent. Your children love you and can benefit from your involvement. Remember, you divorced your spouse, not your children! Make the time you have with your children quality time. Many noncustodial parents jump through hoops trying to keep the children entertained during visits; thus, the term "Disneyland Dad." But being the entertainer doesn't necessarily mean quality time. And this role can infuriate your ex because you can be seen by your children as the fun parent, while the custodial parent remains the one who has to discipline and impose restrictions on them.

A walk in the park, cooking meals together, and having meaningful discussions can be of more quality than the latest film or a trip to the video arcade. Talk with your children on how to spend your time together. Get everyone's ideas.

ON BEING A SINGLE PARENT

Some people become single parents due to the death of a spouse, some choose to have children and remain single, but most single-parent families are the result of divorce. Authors Jane Nelsen, Cheryl Erwin, and Carol Delzer, in their book *Positive Discipline for Single Parents,* point out: "Single parenting is a kind of 'parenting plus': you face all the everyday tasks of raising children, plus the problems of doing a job alone that was originally designed for two people."[6]

Many single parents try to be both mother and father—an impossible, discouraging task. The truth is that one caring, encouraging adult can help children grow up mentally healthy. Children do benefit from a close relationship with an adult the same sex as the absent parent, but he or she doesn't always have to be the other parent. If that parent is not available, relatives, friends, teachers, Big Brothers, and Big Sisters can all provide good role models for children.[7]

Women who are custodial parents may have a problem with money. This certainly makes the job more challenging but not impossible. You do the best you can with what you have. Nelsen, Erwin, and Delzer give some ideas for dealing with financial problems.[8]

- Start with learning how to budget. What do you actually need, and what can be let go until better times? And don't be concerned if your children don't have all the things other children have; you can't afford it, they may gripe, but they'll survive. Involve the children in planning the budget. In your family meetings, discuss what money you have, what is needed, and how much things cost. As with other issues in families, children are more committed if they share in decisions.
- Realize that you may be single but you're not alone. You can network with other single parents—sharing houses, baby-sitting, carpooling, shopping. Perhaps there are single-parent groups or organizations in your community that can help. Check with churches and social agencies.
- If you lack job skills, get them. A community college usually has courses that cost little. You can begin small, one course a semester, for example.
- You may have to go on welfare for a while or ask your parents for help. For many, this is demeaning. But realize that it may be a temporary step that you have to take.
- Finally, examine your feelings and any negative thinking. Pity or anger at your ex—or society—won't help you. Such emotions only sap your energy. Focus on your challenges.

Your Children's Other Parent

We said this before, but we want to say it again: The parents divorced; the children didn't. Your children have a biological and psychological bond with both parents. It is hoped that both parents are willing to be involved with the children and that the involvement is positive. If you attempt to interfere with your children's bond with their other parent, you're asking for trouble; the children will resent you for it.

Jack's ten-year-old son, Billy, spent time with him on the weekends. Jack had the habit of making critical remarks about his ex-spouse to his son.

One weekend, Jack went to pick up Billy. His ex-wife met Jack at the door and told him Billy had gone off to play with friends. "What's this all about? He knows I come to get him each week at this time," Jack said.

Keeping calm, his ex replied, "He told me he didn't like it when you criticized me."

"What . . . oh, come on now. I'm sure you say things about me to him."

"No, actually, Jack, I don't."

"Well, you should have called me."

"I tried to get Billy to talk to you about it, but he's afraid."

"Afraid of me? I can't believe it!"

Jack is reaping what he sowed. He needs to call Billy, talk to him about it, and make sure he stops the criticism.

Family Meetings and Single-Parent Families

Single-parent homes require the utmost cooperation and coordination. Your availability is limited, which means that the children have to take on more responsibility. This increased responsibility can give them a sense of increased self-esteem, since they are now important in making the family function better.

The family meeting is essential to single-parent families. Establishing family routines and responsibilities and planning family fun are best done with the help of the children. Begin the meetings by telling your children how much you need their help. For example, you may be working or going to college, and you may not be home when they get home from school. What will they do after school? Where will they go? If they stay home, what are ways to ensure their safety? What could they do to prepare for dinner so that you're not overwhelmed when you get home? How can they help make things run smoothly? Post a list of the decisions on who does what and when.

Dealing with Differences in Parenting Styles

Chances are that you and your ex had disagreements about things like discipline when you were married. Now that you're divorced, agreement probably has not increased; in fact, you may disagree even more.

A major source of disagreement between ex-spouses usually involves the area of discipline. When you're with your children, you're totally responsible for discipline. When they're with your ex, she or he has to deal with the children as he or she sees fit. Interference on your part will produce tension in the children. If you think your ex's methods are discouraging the children, you may want to discuss the problem with your ex. Use the negotiation skills you've learned in this book to seek an agreement. If you can't reach one, put your effort into your own relationship with your children. Your positive influence can offset negative influences from your ex.[9]

> John had custody of his eight-year-old daughter, Margie, who visited her mother, Dorothy, on weekends. John had been attending a parent study group where he learned about logical consequences. He'd been giving Margie choices for about two months and found her becoming more responsible.

Dorothy, on the other hand, was very strict and yelled at Margie if she didn't do what Dorothy wanted. Margie would come home crying, and it would take a couple of days before John could get her back into the routine of responsibility.

John decided to talk to Dorothy. He invited her for coffee and explained what he was trying to do with Margie, what the results were, and asked for her help. At first Dorothy was skeptical, but she agreed to experiment with the methods John described.

If Dorothy had refused to cooperate with John, he could decide that Margie needed to learn to deal with her mother. He could help Margie by discussing some ways Margie could get along with Dorothy better. As we said above, children have to learn to get along with all kinds of people. Of course, if you suspect child abuse, you'll need to contact the proper authorities.

Dating and Remarriage

Your social and sexual life doesn't necessarily end when you divorce. In fact, some divorced people engage in casual sexual affairs to prove to themselves that they're still sexually attractive. Bringing casual partners into the home can confuse and frighten children.[10]

Many single parents remarry. When a relationship is serious, the children need to be notified. A frank discussion of your intentions and listening to their feelings is essential. Remember, most children fantasize about their parents getting back together. A stepparent is often seen as an intrusion. Assure them that they will still have the same relationship with their other parent and that the stepparent is not a substitute but an addition to the family. Be open about your relationship with your intended and explain that he or she will be sleeping with you. You'll find your children more accepting if they know what to expect.

LIVING IN A STEPFAMILY

Another name for stepfamilies is "blended families," which implies that you take two families and "blend" them together. However, we think our colleague Dr. Kevin Leman, a renowned author on parenting, offers the best explanation of the term: "Stepfamily members often feel as if they're in a blender, turning green from getting whirled violently around and around while they're being chopped to pieces in the process."[11]

This couldn't be closer to the truth; living in a stepfamily is challenging! And the family is never blended. It's always in the process of blending; there's not a finished product.

One of the biggest mistakes stepfamily parents make is buying into society's expectations that because they're a two-parent family they're like a nuclear family. A nuclear family involves two original parents to whom the children are biologically bonded. Obviously this isn't true of stepchildren. Relationships grow slowly in stepfamilies. Love's not like coffee; it's not instant!

As a stepfamily, you will have to establish new relationships—as a couple and as parents. New relationships require adjustments and compromises and can be painful at times. The adjustment period begins in courtship.

Courtship is the time to resolve the emotional issues from your past relationships. If these issues aren't resolved, you may find yourself entering into a relationship mirroring what you had before; without sincere self-examination, people tend to make the same mistakes. Even if you haven't been married before, your new intended may be attracted to traits in you that are similar to those of his or her ex-spouse—and may not even be aware of it. So how can this mistake be avoided? Premarital counseling can help both of you examine your relationship and point out pitfalls and possibilities. And it's a good idea to eventually involve the children in the counseling to sort out issues.

Premarital counseling can help, but it's not a panacea. There's no guarantee that you and your spouse won't carry expectations from previous relationships into your marriage.

Therefore, as in any marriage, it's especially important that you learn to accept each other's weaknesses and appreciate each other's strengths.

Multiple Relationships

There are multiple relationships in a stepfamily. First and foremost is the couple relationship. Then there is the relationship between biological parents and biological children, between stepparents and stepchildren, between grandparents and step-grandparents, and finally, between stepsiblings.

The Couple Relationship

The couple relationship is complicated by the immediate presence of children. Unlike most first marriages, the couple doesn't have a private adjustment period; the new couple must be parents from the start. Still, you need to take time as a couple to nurture your relationship; date nights and weekends away can help. Marriage-enrichment courses can also assist the new couple. In short, if your marriage isn't strong, your success as a stepfamily will become jeopardized.

Keep in mind that the children don't have the investment in your marriage that you do. They may even try to separate you! Why? Because most stepchildren didn't want the situation in the first place. They remain committed to the original family and see the stepparent as an intruder. With that in mind, it's extremely important that you work hard to make a strong marital bond.

Realize that you don't need the approval of the children for your marriage. Your decision to marry is your decision. The children will have to learn to adjust, and they can learn, just as they learn to adjust to many other things in their lives.

Tom and Carol were newly married. The family included Susan, thirteen, Joe, ten, from Tom's previous marriage, and Carol's daughter, Brenda, eight. The children were constantly bickering and complaining. Brenda would complain to her mother that Joe picked on her. Carol took her daughter's case to her husband. Susan, Tom's daughter, stuck up for her brother by accusing Carol of favoring Brenda.

Tom tried to smooth things over by protecting his new stepdaughter. This, of course, infuriated Joe, causing more attacks on Brenda and more protection from Carol and complaints from Susan.

Finally, Tom and Carol got into it, blaming each other for their biological children's problems. The children picked up on this, and the fights escalated.

Tom's and Carol's children were vying for power and doing their best to be disruptive. By protecting Brenda and engaging in conflict themselves, the parents made things worse. If Tom and Carol had let the children work out their own relationships, they would have found the children eventually adjusting to each other and the new situation because there would be no payoff for disrupting the family.

Relationships with Your Biological Children

Like Tom in our example, biological parents can bend over backward to not show favoritism to their own children. This backfires because your biological children will resent it and your stepchildren will take advantage of it. Other stepparents, like Carol, stick up for their biological children at their stepchildren's expense. So how do you get out of this situation? First, realize that your bond with your biological child is usually stronger than your bond with your stepchildren—this is natural—so don't fight it by trying to overcompensate. Don't play into it either by favoring your own children. Do your best to treat the children equally and let it go at that. Most of all, don't interfere in the children's relationships with each other. They will learn to adjust to each other.

Relationships with Your Stepchildren

Stepparents get along best with their stepchildren when they establish their own unique relationship with them. Don't try to replace their absent parent. They'll resent it, and you'll have nothing but trouble. Don't expect instant love or cooperation. Relationships take time to develop.

Many stepparents bend over backward to gain their stepchildren's acceptance. They may try too hard and expect something in return. The harder they try, the more resistance they may get.

Stepparents sometimes try to outdo the absent biological parent by becoming the better cook, the better companion, or the better provider of material things. These behaviors backfire as well. The children will either take advantage of it or resent it.

Here's another problem: The biological parent in the family may feel guilty because his or her children won't respond to the new parent. The children catch on to this and may become manipulative. Conflict may develop in a war between the generations. At some point the parents may realize that they're losing the war and attempt to gain the kids' approval either by attempting to please them or by becoming their servants. Then the parents tire of the tyrannical situation and attempt to reestablish control, only to find the battle raging on.[12] The family meeting can help in these situations. We'll discuss family meetings and stepfamilies shortly, but first we want to address the issue of stepsibling relationships.

Stepsibling Relationships

Helping stepsiblings integrate into the new family unit can be a real challenge. Remember, in most cases the children didn't decide to become a part of this new family.

Keep in mind that each child in the new family is trying to find his or her place. You can help all your children by focusing on their strengths and using their talents to contribute to the family as a whole, helping them feel unique as well as important. Is one of them a good cook? Another a good organizer? Do you have a Mr. or Ms. Fixit?

The family-constellation position of each child must be considered. Remember that the family constellation (see chapter 1) is a major influence on a person's lifestyle. If your and/or your spouse's children are older when you marry, their lifestyles will be pretty well set. The two youngest, for example, will likely continue to compete for the special spot regardless of who's the younger of the two. That's why it's important to take each child's family-constellation position into consideration as you go about "blending" your new family.

You may have two eldest children who can set up a struggle for power if not handled appropriately. In this case, it's important to encourage cooperation to make the new family work. Tell them how much they are needed in meeting the increased responsibilities in the new family. Encourage their leadership abilities in generating ideas for running an efficient household. The emphasis is on their cooperation, that is, coming to mutually agreeable solutions, not who's got the best idea.

Second children, you will recall, often strive to overtake the eldest. They can be particularly social if the eldest takes the more task-oriented role. If this is the case, you can encourage their social skills by having them bring ideas of fun things to do together to the family meeting. If there's been a role reversal and the second born is psychologically older, then he or she can contribute in much the same way as an eldest child would.

Middle children are often concerned with fairness and they may have difficulty fitting into a stepfamily in which there are more children's rights to consider. They may see things as increasingly unfair—the divorce and remarriage were unfair in the first place. This further confirms to them how unfair life is. While you can't ensure that things will be totally fair for them in the new family—that's a false picture of life, anyway—you can focus on their sense of fairness as a strength. A concern with fairness can also mean being able to see both sides. These children are often the peacemakers of the world.[13] In family meetings, for example, they can be asked to come up with fair ways to distribute chores.

Having two youngest in a stepfamily can be challenging. Each one is used to being the baby and the center of attention. They may be demanding and rebellious. They need a lot of encouragement for their cooperation. Look for ways they can contribute and let them know you appreciate it. Don't reinforce misbehavior; use ignoring and consequences where appropriate.

An only child—or two—thrust into a stepfamily can upset you as well as the child. Like youngests, these children are used to being the center of attention. But it's more than that; they are used to being the "one and only." Now they have new children to contend with. Remember that "onlys" often have characteristics of eldests as well as youngests. They can be strivers, wanting to be first, just like the eldests. So they can lock horns with both the eldest and the youngest of the new family. Watch out for their manipulation skills; they may try to drive a wedge between you and your new spouse. They may try to separate out their own parent and try to continue the exclusive relationship with him or her they had when that parent was single. How do you deal with this? Work at involving them in the new family. The secret to integrating them into the new family is using their creativity to foster cooperation. They can be paired with the eldest, for example, to come up with ways to make the family function better.

Family Meetings and Stepfamilies

The most effective way to operate in a stepfamily is the same as operating in any other family—democratically. The family meeting provides a forum for all to be heard and for decisions to be made. With family meetings, a feeling of belonging to the new family unit can emerge. Each family member learns how she or he can best fit into the new structure. Cooperation can be gained through focusing on using each member's strengths to contribute to the family.

Like single-parent families, stepfamilies often involve complex schedules. As in many families, both parents often work outside the home. There are visitations with the other biological parents and possibly another stepparent and stepsiblings to consider. If joint custody is involved, there are plans to be made to include new family members for extended periods of time. Budgets in stepfamilies are often tight, as parents may have to partially support two families. All these things make family meetings in stepfamilies vital.

Discipline Decisions

Stepparents often bring different parenting styles to their new families. One may be very autocratic; the other, quite permissive. The goal is to work out a mutually acceptable style, if possible. If it isn't possible, then agree to disagree and each establish his or her own relationship with the children. Agree to not interfere in the other's discipline decisions (child abuse excepted, of course). The process of exploring alternatives that you learned in chapter 6 can help you and your spouse negotiate your differences.

Until a stepparent's relationship with the stepchildren is on good footing, it's best for the biological parent to deal with discipline issues with his or her own children. Stepchildren won't accept discipline from a stepparent until there's a positive relationship. Also, even though a biological parent may initially want the stepparent to take over the burden of discipline, the biological parent may resent it if she or he doesn't agree with the stepparent's methods.

An exception to the biological parent's handling discipline with his or her own children is when there are problems between the stepparent and the stepchildren. At that point, they own the problem. For example, a child speaks in a disrespectful way to the stepparent. Another exception is when the stepparent is left in charge while the biological parent is absent. The biological parent informs the children of this gradually so that they become used to the idea.

Finally, as the stepparent develops a good relationship with the stepchildren through encouragement and spending quality time with them, the stepparent becomes equally responsible for discipline. How long this takes depends on the people involved.

While you're establishing the atmosphere of your new family, you'll get complaints from your own children about how your spouse is treating them. Don't set yourself up as judge and jury. They have to learn how to get along with their new parent—tell them so. Do listen to them, however, and explore alternatives to help them develop ways to get along better with your spouse. If you have concerns about how your spouse is treating your children, tell him or her so in private. Negotiate your differences.

You'll both be more effective if you follow the disciplinary procedures of I-messages and natural and logical consequences you've learned in this book. But if what you're reading makes sense to you and not your spouse, you'll need to agree to disagree. Remember, you can still make a difference in your children's lives even if your spouse disagrees. In this way, the stepfamily is no different from any other parenting situation.

Preventing Another Divorce

Stepfamilies may get themselves into trouble by postponing dealing with problems until they become a crisis. Dealing with problems as they arise—or better yet, if you can anticipate them—will help prevent crises. Encouragement, communication, family meetings, and exploring alternatives are skills that can help you deal with issues before they reach a crisis state. If things aren't working for you, it's time to seek professional help. When seeking help, don't be afraid to ask a counselor if she or he has had experience in working with stepfamilies. Shop around; ask friends, your doctor, your minister.

CONCLUSION

Dealing with divorce, being a single parent, or living in a stepfamily are all challenging situations. But millions of people manage in these situations. (By the year 2000, it is estimated that single-parent families and stepfamilies will outnumber nuclear families!) They have their rewards as well as their difficulties.

In this chapter we've discussed the uniqueness of each structure and how your new skills can be applied. More detailed discussion is beyond the scope of this book. Therefore, we suggest the following books if you need more information:

Blau, Melinda. 1995. *Families Apart: Ten Keys to Successful Co-Parenting.* New York: Perigee.

Cohen, Miriam Galper. 1991. *The Joint Custody Handbook: Creating Arrangements That Work.* Philadelphia, Penn.: Running Press.

Coleman, William L. 1993. *StepTrouble: A Survival Guide for Teenagers with Stepparents.* Minneapolis, Minn.: Comp-Care.

Dinkmeyer, Don, Gary D. McKay, and Joyce L. McKay. 1987. *New Beginnings: Skills for Single Parents and Stepfamily Parents, Parent's Manual.* Champaign, Ill.: Research Press. Available from Research Press, (217) 352-3273.

Kimball, Gayle. 1994. *How to Survive Your Parents' Divorce: Kids' Advice to Kids.* Chico, Calif.: Equality=Press.

Lansky, Vicki. 1989. *Vicki Lansky's Divorce Book for Parents.* New York: Signet.

Leman, Kevin. 1994. *Living in a Stepfamily without Getting Stepped On.* Nashville, Tenn.: Thomas Nelson.

Nelsen, Jane, Cheryl Erwin, and Carol Delzer. 1994. *Positive Discipline for Single Parents.* Rocklin, Calif.: Prima.

APPENDIX A: THE
TROUBLESHOOTING GUIDE

Occasionally you may try out a method specifically illustrated in this book and experience failure. When such failure occurs, carefully analyze the situation. First, write down exactly what you did and how the child responded. Second, use the following checklist to guide your investigation. When you determine the source(s) of the difficulty, reread the section(s) describing the procedure involved. Be sure to read the reference(s) completely as you may have misunderstood more than one aspect of the procedure or procedures.

General Principles

Did I talk too much?
Did I "shout with my mouth shut"?
Did I choose the appropriate approach?
Did I assume ownership of the child's problem (either during a listening session or with a problem where the consequences would occur outside the parent-child relationship)?
Did I neglect to encourage positive behavior?

Did I spend some friendly time with my child?
Did my tone of voice imply respect for the child?
Was I consistent?
Did I remain firm as well as kind?

For Problems Involving Use of Communication Skills

Did I truly listen or was I just saying words?
Did I misuse reflective listening through trying to manipulate or criticize?
Did I enter into exploring alternatives too soon?
Did I overdo reflective listening and/or exploring alternatives?
Did my I-message focus on my feelings, or did I actually send disguised you-messages?
Did I overdo I-messages?
Did I enter problem solving with preconceived solutions? Did I try to manipulate during the problem-solving session? Did I take enough time to listen, explore alternatives, or problem-solve?

For Problems Involving Consequences

Was my logical consequence truly logical and related to the misbehavior?
Did I use the correct timing?
Did I try to control with consequences? Did I truly allow the child to choose and accept his choice?
Did I use a logical consequence in a situation where a natural consequence was more appropriate?

For Problems Involving the Family Meeting

Did I violate agreements made in family meetings?
Did I violate any principles or procedures of the family meeting?

APPENDIX B: THE PROBLEM-ANALYSIS AND CORRECTION GUIDE

The following guide will help you analyze your interactions with your child. Combined with the "Troubleshooting Guide" in Appendix A, the guide will help discover solutions to your child training challenges.

GUIDE	COMMENTS
1. The incident.	Describe exactly what the child did. You may wish to include the time and place.
2. My action.	Describe your feelings and exactly what you said and/or did.
3. My child's reaction.	Describe exactly how the child responded to what you did—facial expressions, words, actions.
4. My child's goal.	Make a guess based on your feelings and his reaction to your attempts to correct him.
5. What principles did I fail to consider?	If you have trouble here, see the list of principles and the "Troubleshooting Guide" in Appendix A.

6. My plan for redirecting his goal:
  a. discouraging the unacceptable behavior
  b. encouraging acceptable behavior
	Describe exactly what you plan to do to correct the misbehavior. Refer to sections on communication, encouragement, consequences, and the family meeting.

7. Results (after at least one week).	Describe exactly what happened as a result of your plan. If not satisfactory, analyze (see "Troubleshooting Guide") and try again.

APPENDIX C: PARENT STUDY GROUPS

Many parents find they learn best when they can discuss new ideas and skills with other parents. You could start a parent study group with *Raising a Responsible Child* as the text. You might begin with a group of friends or at your children's school or your church.

Here are some guidelines for the study group:

- Meet once a week. Study a chapter each week.
- Rotate the leadership. Each person in the group takes a turn at being responsible for discussing the chapter. He or she can prepare questions for the group to discuss.
- Make the book the authority. Don't get sidetracked with group members' favorite parenting theories. The purpose of the group is to learn what the book has to offer. A typical question can be: "What does the book say about this issue?"
- Include in your discussion how to apply what you're learning to your own children. It can be interesting to discuss ideas, but nothing will happen unless people are willing to put the ideas into practice.

- Discuss the results of each person's efforts at the beginning of each meeting.

You may wish to join a more formal parent study group. We have developed structured groups called the STEP (Systematic Training for Effective Parenting) programs. STEP is the most widely used parenting program in the world. There are four STEP programs:

> STEP. This program is designed for parents of children from age six to preteens.
> Early Childhood STEP. This program applies the principles of STEP to children under six.
> STEP/Teen. This program is for parents of preteens and teenagers.
> The Next STEP. This is an advanced program. It's for parents who've completed one of the other STEP programs.

Each STEP program has a parenting text:
STEP: *The Parent's Handbook.*
Early Childhood STEP: *Parenting Young Children.*
STEP/teen: *Parenting Teenagers.*
The Next STEP: *The Effective Parent.*
The first three books are available in the bookstores. The last book, *The Effective Parent,* is available only from American Guidance Service ([1-800] 328-2560).

Each STEP program has a leader's manual and a video for practicing skills. The leader takes the group through a step-by-step lesson sequence. The emphasis is on understanding and applying the program's principles in group members' families.

If you're a single parent or a stepparent, you may be interested in New Beginnings: Skills for Single Parents and Stepfamily Parents. This program applies the ideas presented in *Raising a Responsible Child* and STEP to these family structures. (The parents' manual from New Beginnings can be purchased from Research Press: [217] 352-3273.)

How do you find these groups? The STEP programs are taught in schools, churches, and counseling agencies. Most likely, the groups are available in your community; a few phone calls will help you locate one. New Beginnings may be more challenging to find. But don't despair, lots of single parents and stepfamily parents participate in STEP groups.

NOTES

CHAPTER 1

1. Rudolf Dreikurs, *Psychology in the Classroom*, 2nd ed. (New York: Harper and Row, 1968).
2. Kevin Leman, *Bringing Up Children Without Tearing Them Down* (New York: Delacorte Press, 1993).
3. Rudolf Dreikurs and Vicki Soltz, *Children: The Challenge* (New York: Dutton, 1964).

CHAPTER 2

1. Don Dinkmeyer, Gary D. McKay, and James S. Dinkmeyer, *Parenting Young Children* (Circle Pines, Minn.: American Guidance Service, 1989).
2. Don Dinkmeyer, Gary D. McKay, Don Dinkmeyer, Jr., James S. Dinkmeyer, and Joyce L. McKay, *The Effective Parent* (Circle Pines, Minn.: American Guidance Service, 1987).
3. Rudolf Dreikurs and Vicki Soltz, *Children: The Challenge* (New York: Dutton, 1964).
4. Rudolf Dreikurs and Loren Grey, *A Parent's Guide to Child Discipline* (New York: Hawthorn Books, 1970).

CHAPTER 3

1. Albert Ellis, *Reason and Emotion in Psychotherapy* (New York: Lyle Stuart, 1962).

CHAPTER 4

1. Kevin Leman, *Bringing Up Kids Without Tearing Them Down* (New York: Delacorte Press, 1993).
2. Harold H. Mosak, "Adlerian Psychotherapy," in *Current Psychotherapies*, 5th ed., Raymond Corsini and Danny Wedding, eds. (Itasca, Ill.: F. E. Peacock, 1995).
3. Gary D. McKay and Oscar C. Christensen, "Helping Adults Change Disjunctive Emotional Responses to Children's Misbehavior," *Journal of Individual Psychology* 34, no. 1 (1978): 82.
4. Rudolf Dreikurs and Vicki Soltz, *Children: The Challenge* (New York: Dutton, 1964).
5. Gary D. McKay, *The Basics of Encouragement* (Coral Springs, Fla.: CMTI Press, 1992) (booklet).

CHAPTER 5

1. Don Dinkmeyer and Gary D. McKay, *The Parent's Handbook (from Systematic Training for Effective Parenting [STEP])*. (Circle Pines, Minn.: American Guidance Service, 1989); distributed in bookstores by Random House.
2. Ibid.
3. Ibid.
4. Don Dinkmeyer and Gary D. McKay, *Parenting Teenagers (from Systematic Training for Effective Parenting of Teens [STEP/Teen])* (Circle Pines, Minn.: American Guidance Service, 1990); distributed in bookstores by Random House.
5. Thomas Gordon, *P.E.T. in Action* (New York: Bantam, 1976).

CHAPTER 6

1. Thomas Gordon, *Parent Effectiveness Training* (New York: Peter H. Wyden, 1970); and Don Dinkmeyer and Gary D. McKay, *Parenting Teenagers* (Circle Pines, Minn.: American Guidance Service, 1990).
2. Dinkmeyer and McKay.
3. Rudolf Dreikurs and Loren Grey, *A Parent's Guide to Child Discipline* (New York: Hawthorn Books, 1970); Dinkmeyer and McKay.

CHAPTER 8

1. Rudolf Dreikurs and Vicki Soltz, *Children: The Challenge* (New York: Dutton, 1964).
2. Rudolf Dreikurs and Loren Grey, *A Parent's Guide to Child Discipline* (New York: Hawthorn Books, 1970).
3. Don Dinkmeyer, Gary D. McKay, and Joyce L. McKay, *New Beginnings: Skills for Single Parents and Stepfamily Parents, Parent's Manual* (Champaign, Ill.: Research Press, 1987); Don Dinkmeyer, and Gary D. McKay, *Parenting Teenagers* (Circle Pines, Minn.: American Guidance Service, 1990); Don Dinkmeyer, Gary D. McKay, and James S. Dinkmeyer, *Parenting Young Children* (Circle Pines, Minn.: American Guidance Service, 1989).

CHAPTER 9

1. Don Dinkmeyer and Gary D. McKay, *Parenting Teenagers* (Circle Pines, Minn.: American Guidance Service, 1990).
2. Ibid.
3. Ibid.
4. Ibid.
5. Joyce L. McKay, Don Dinkmeyer, Jr., and Don Dinkmeyer, Sr., *Drug Free 2: A Drug Use Prevention Program for Grades 4–6* (Circle Pines, Minn.: American Guidance Service, 1992).
6. Gary D. McKay, Joyce L. McKay, and Don Dinkmeyer, *STEP for Substance Abuse Prevention* (Circle Pines, Minn.: American Guidance Service, 1990).
7. Dinkmeyer and McKay.
8. Jane Nelsen, Lynn Lott, and H. Stephen Glenn, *Positive Discipline A-Z: 1001 Solutions to Everyday Parenting Problems* (Rocklin, Calif.: Prima, 1993).
9. Ibid.
10. Stanley I. Greenspan and Jacqueline Salmon, *Playground Politics: Understanding the Emotional Life of Your School-Age Child* (New York: Addison-Wesley, 1993).
11. Ibid.
12. Ted Koppel (host), *Nightline Town Meeting: Teens and Sex: What'll We Tell the Kids?* New York, American Broadcasting Corporation, February 17, 1995.
13. Dinkmeyer and McKay.
14. McKay, McKay, and Dinkmeyer.

CHAPTER 10

1. Elisabeth Kübler-Ross, *On Death and Dying* (New York: Macmillan, 1969).
2. Don Dinkmeyer, Gary D. McKay, and Joyce L. McKay, *New Beginnings: Skills for Single Parents and Stepfamily Parents, Parent's Manual* (Champaign, Ill.: Research Press, 1987).
3. Ibid.
4. Vicki Lansky, *Vicki Lansky's Divorce Book for Parents* (New York: Signet, 1991).
5. Ibid.
6. Jane Nelsen, Cheryl Erwin, and Carol Delzer, *Positive Discipline for Single Parents* (Rocklin, Calif.: Prima Publishing, 1994), 1.
7. Dinkmeyer, McKay, and McKay.
8. Nelsen, Erwin, and Delzer.
9. Dinkmeyer, McKay, and McKay.
10. Ibid.
11. Kevin Leman, *Living in a Stepfamily Without Getting Stepped On* (Nashville, Tenn.: Thomas Nelson, 1994), 9.
12. Dinkmeyer, McKay, and McKay.
13. Leman.

INDEX

Printed in the United States
1258000002B/1-57